THE FAMILY HANDYMAN®
PRACTICAL BOOK
OF SAVING HOME ENERGY

Editors, THE FAMILY HANDYMAN

TAB BOOKS

BLUE RIDGE SUMMIT, PA. 17214

FIRST EDITION

FIRST PRINTING—NOVEMBER 1978

Copyright © 1978 by TAB BOOKS

Printed in the United States of America

Library of Congress Cataloging in Publication Data

Tab Books.
    The family handyman practical book of saving home energy.

    Includes index.
    1. Dwellings—Energy conservation. I. Title.
TJ163.5.D86T3   696   78-10704
ISBN 0-8306-9871-X
ISBN 0-8306-1109-6 pbk.

THE FAMILY HANDYMAN® is a trademark of The Webb Company, trademark registered in U.S. Patent and Trademark Office.

Cover photo courtesy of The Family Handyman

THE FAMILY HANDYMAN® PRACTICAL BOOK OF SAVING HOME ENERGY

Contents

ACKNOWLEDGEMENTS

We extend our thanks to the many professionals who contributed to the publication of this book. We thank especially Tom Philbin, who assembled the final manuscript, as well as Terry Redlin, Ron Chamberlain, Lorn Manthey, Mort Schultz, Lars Nelson, Greg Northcutt and Rose Gross. We appreciate the valuable advice and counsel of Spencer Young, Minnegasco; the Gas Appliance Manufacturers Association; the Minnesota Energy Agency; Ron Scott and Robert LeChevalier of the U.S. Department of Energy. We also thank the many companies and organizations we worked with for the suggestions and materials which made this book possible.

Editors, THE FAMILY HANDYMAN ®

Chapter 1

You Can Become an Energy Expert

You Can Become an Energy Expert

Never before has the American public been so conscious of saving energy. Hardly a day goes by that you don't hear about our dwindling energy supplies. Each year homeowners across the country find that the costs of home energy, regardless of form, have risen sharply again (Fig. 1-1). This book shows you dozens of ways to get the most from each dollar you spend on energy.

As a homeowner, you can save hundreds of dollars a year by being energy-smart, often without investing a great deal of money. Just by fixing leaky faucets and keeping radiators clean, for example, you can save hundreds of dollars during the life of a home.

UNDERSTANDING ENERGY LOSSES

How can you become a home energy expert? First take time to understand the ordinary ways in which home energy is wasted. Think of your home as a porous structure. According to the laws of physics, heat always migrates to a cooler area. This means that, in winter, heated air inside your home attempts to escape outside. In summer, warm outside air attempts to penetrate the home structure. The longer that heating and cooling equipment has to work to compensate for this movement of air, the more energy is used, and the higher your energy bills.

The "porosity" of your home is the most important key to saving energy dollars. The better your home is sealed, the less

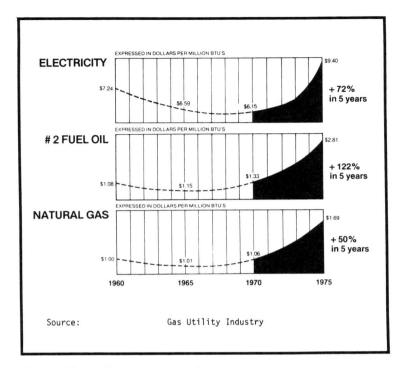

Fig. 1-1. History of home energy costs.

infiltration will occur, and the less fuel you will need to use. Figure 1-2 gives typical infiltration figures.

You can seal your home in a variety of ways. The most important way, by far, is with insulation. This material is designed to resist the passage of heat through it. The more fully you meet the maximum requirements experts specify for your home, the more money you are going to save. Caulking and weatherstripping are two other major materials you can use to seal structural cracks and openings around windows and doors.

Windows and doors represent critical areas to be sealed. Made of glass, wood and metal, windows are solid. But they are also porous (to a greater or lesser degree). Besides sealing around these units to reduce air flow, you can use storm doors and storm windows and double- and triple-glazed windows to provide dead air spaces for resisting the flow of heat.

Heating and cooling equipment, however, are the core of any energy saving program. Heating equipment, especially, should be maintained in good working order. Like a car that isn't tuned properly, equipment that isn't maintained properly will waste fuel.

There are many significant methods to save energy, and we point them out in the rest of this book. Even if you only accomplish the most basic of them, you will have progressed a long way along the road to making appreciable savings and increasing the comfort of your home.

DOWN TO BUSINESS

With or without government help, homeowners across the country are realizing benefits from making their homes weatherproof. The amount of insulation used in the average new home, for example, was only 500 lbs. in 1967, and experts predict that this figure will rise to more than 900 by 1980 (Fig. 1-3). In 1973 only 15% of the homes in America had attic insulation of 6″ or more. By 1977 the percentage of houses with 6″ or more of attic insulation rose to 32.2%, and the percentage has continued to rise rapidly since then. In fact, as Fig. 1-4 shows, during 1974, 1975 and 1976 eight million American homeowners added attic insulation.

Because of the high interest in improving the energy efficiency of the average home, researchers began investigating the economics of various energy-saving measures which a homeowner could take. Initial studies indicate that although some projects are

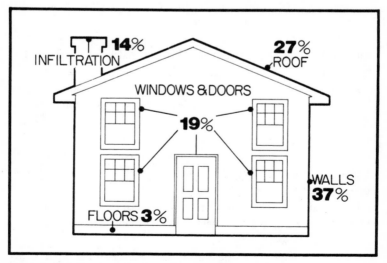

Fig. 1-2. Air infiltration rates in various parts of the house.

14

AVERAGE POUNDS OF INSULATION PER NEW HOUSING UNIT			
	SINGLE FAMILY OWNER OCCUPIED	MULTI-FAMILY	MOBILE
1967	467	235	200
1974	624	314	512
1976	721	321	659
1980	900+	371	810

(BASED ON 1600 SQ. FT. PER SINGLE FAMILY UNIT, 1,031 SQ. FT PER MULTI-FAMILY UNIT, AND 962 SQ. FT. PER MOBILE UNIT)

SOURCE: U.S. DEPARTMENT OF COMMERCE, OWENS-CORNING

Fig. 1-3. More and more American homeowners are insulating their houses.

more economically attractive than others, nearly all are good investments. The acts of adding insulation, storm windows, and weatherstripping, and placing heating equipment in proper operation are all projected to provide a payback within 10 years or less (Fig. 1-5).

In specific tests conducted by Chevron USA, a professional furnace tune-up demonstrated the best payback (Fig. 1-6). Next highest payback came from replacing an older, inefficient furnace burner with a new one. Third best return came from installing a

ATTIC REINSULATION 1974-75-76			
INSULATION THICKNESS	HOMES REINSULATING 1974-76	ATTIC INSULATION LEVELS AS OF JANUARY 1, 1977	
	HOMES (IN THOUSANDS)	HOMES (IN THOUSANDS)	PERCENT OF TOTAL HOMES
0"	2,286	1,908	4.6
Less than 4"	2,745	11,380	27.3
4" – 5"	1,755	14,953	35.9
6" and more	1,202	13,468	32.2
	7,988	41,709*	

* Reflects 1,988,000 net homes (owner-occupied) added since 1974 survey.
Source: Owens-Corning

Fig. 1-4. By 1977 nearly one-third of U.S. houses had 6" or more of attic insulation.

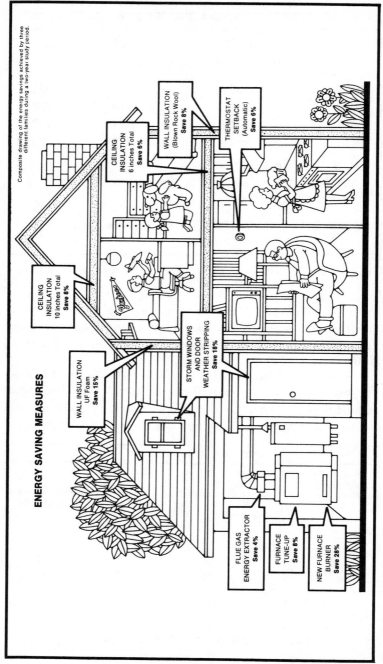

Composite drawing of the energy savings achieved by three different families during a two-year study period.

ENERGY SAVING MEASURES

CEILING INSULATION 6 inches Total **Save 6%**

WALL INSULATION (Blown Rock Wool) **Save 8%**

THERMOSTAT SETBACK (Automatic) **Save 6%**

CEILING INSULATION 10 inches Total **Save 8%**

WALL INSULATION UF Foam **Save 15%**

STORM WINDOWS AND DOOR WEATHER STRIPPING **Save 18%**

FLUE GAS ENERGY EXTRACTOR **Save 4%**

FURNACE TUNE-UP **Save 8%**

NEW FURNACE BURNER **Save 28%**

Fig. 1-5. The economics of energy conservation at home.

LOCATION	MEASURED OIL SAVING, %	PREDICTED ENERGY SAVING, %	MEASURED ENERGY SAVING, %	PAYBACK TIME, * YEARS	RATE OF RETURN,* %	CONTRACTOR INSTALLED COST, $
PORTLAND:						
FURNACE TUNE-UP	5	6	8	1	96	38
CEILING INSULATION, 10-IN. TOTAL	9	7	8	6	18	218
THERMOSTAT SETBACK (AUTOMATIC)	18	13	6	4	29	102
WALL INSULATION (UF FOAM)	28	23	19	8	14	488
FLUE GAS ENERGY EXTRACTOR		6				135
						981
SEATTLE:						
CEILING INSULATION, 6-IN. TOTAL	4	7	6	6	17	114
STORM WINDOWS AND DOOR WEATHER STRIPPING	23	14	18	7	15	708
						822
SPOKANE:						
CEILING INSULATION, 10-IN. TOTAL	11	9	8	8	13	298
WALL INSULATION (BLOWN ROCK WOOL)	13	21	8	15	5	520
NEW FURNACE BURNER	36	23	28	2	44	310
						1119

*BASED ON MEASURED ENERGY SAVING IN TESTS CONDUCTED BY CHEVRON USA, 1977.
NOTE: EACH PERCENTAGE SAVING IS WITH RESPECT TO THE TEST HOME'S CONDITION
IMMEDIATELY PRIOR TO THE MODIFICATION.

Fig. 1-6. A professional furnace tune-up yields the best payback.

chimney heat reclaimer. This is a device that extracts waste heat from the exhaust stack of a furnace. Automatic set-back thermostats that lower settings during the night and raise them during the day also showed appreciable savings.

Ceiling insulation in this test showed a relatively long payback period because some insulation already existed in the ceilings. If ceilings are totally uninsulated, the payback period is much shorter. Insulating walls, while it would appear to provide an excellent opportunity to save energy, actually showed up as one of the least attractive projects from a dollar-return standpoint. Reasons include the high expense of installation, plus the difficulty of insulating walls properly after a house has been built.

The payback period for any energy-saving project will vary regionally. In more moderate climates, storm doors may show low payback characteristics if considered only from an energy standpoint. But if you need a screen door for summer use, and opt for a combination screen/storm door, roughly half the cost can be charged off as screen door usage. Recovering half the cost of the door in energy savings then becomes economically feasible.

Two things should be kept in mind when considering energy efficiency standards. First, building codes—even those of the federal government—are *minimal* requirements, not the optimum for best energy efficiency. Many state and local codes hark back to the days when it was cheaper to burn large amounts of low-cost fuel than to try to conserve. Secondly, any computation of payback resulting from steps you take to save energy will depend on a number of factors, including inflation rates, energy costs, and how intensively you've tried to save energy.

As pointed out, adding insulation to an insulation-less home will provide higher returns than if insulation is added to a home already containing some.

WEATHERPROOFING YOUR HOME

A number of companies and utilities have spent much time and effort in designing energy efficient homes. By examining the features incorporated into these homes, you can gain an understanding of what contributes to energy conservation (Fig. 1-7). Many of the features can be duplicated in your own home.

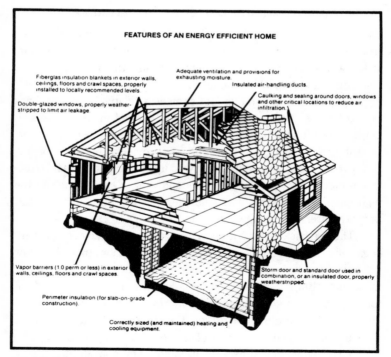

FEATURES OF AN ENERGY EFFICIENT HOME

Fiberglas insulation blankets in exterior walls, ceilings, floors and crawl spaces, properly installed to locally recommended levels.

Double-glazed windows, properly weather-stripped to limit air leakage.

Adequate ventilation and provisions for exhausting moisture.

Insulated air-handling ducts.

Caulking and sealing around doors, windows and other critical locations to reduce air infiltration.

Vapor barriers (1.0 perm or less) in exterior walls, ceilings, floors and crawl spaces.

Perimeter insulation (for slab-on-grade construction).

Storm door and standard door used in combination, or an insulated door, properly weatherstripped.

Correctly sized (and maintained) heating and cooling equipment.

Fig. 1-7. What a house needs to give you the most for your energy dollar.

How Does Your Home Score?

1 Six inches (R-19) or more of attic insulation
Yes = 2 pts.; No = – 1 pt. _____

2 Insulation in floor over unheated crawl space
Yes = 1 pt.; No = 0 pt. _____

3 Storm windows & doors
Yes = 1 pt.; No. = 0 pt. _____

4 Caulking & weatherstripping around windows & doors
Yes = 1 pt.; No. = 0 pt. _____

5 Minimum 3½ inches (R-11) insulation in sidewalls
Yes = 1 pt.; No = – 1 pt. _____

6 Insulation basement walls
Yes = 1 pt.; No = 0 pt. _____

7 Adequate attic ventilation
Yes = 1 pt.; No = 0 pt. _____

8 Light colored roof (in warm climates)
Yes = 1 pt.; No = 0 pt. _____

9 Shaded lot
Yes = 1 pt.; No = 0 pt. _____

10 Properly maintained and adjusted heating and cooling equipment
Yes = 1 pt.; No = 0 pt. _____

Total _____

If your home scores 10 points or better, your fuel bills are well under control. A score of 5 to 10 means your home may benefit from selective energy-saving improvements, such as increased insulation, more storm windows and doors. Scores below 5 mean heating and cooling dollars are being wasted.

Fig. 1-8. A test for evaluating the energy efficiency of your house.

The actual cost of weatherproofing your home will depend on many variables, such as climate, your home's construction, and whether you are making improvements from scratch or have already taken steps to make your home energy efficient. How can you ultimately save? The Division of Energy, U.S. Department of Housing and Urban Development (HUD), says that by properly insulating your home you can cut your yearly heating and air conditioning costs as much as 30%.

The best bet is to study each conservation measure separately, and in the context of your own energy saving program. Check with materials suppliers, state and federal energy agencies, and utilities before you invest your dollars. The listing which follows will give you a general idea of what you can expect to save. It was compiled by the American Society of Heating, Refrigerating and Air-Conditioning Engineers, Inc. All the steps are recommended by ASHRAE, a non-profit professional organization.

See Fig. 1-8 for a quiz about the energy efficiency of your own home.

MEASURES WHICH COST NOTHING

Step	Cost	Annual Savings	Comments
Turn down thermostat, especially at night or when house is unoccupied; keep it lower than you are used to	0	A 5° reduction from 10 p.m. to 6 a.m. will save 8% in Minneapolis, 11% in Dallas	Savings depend on weather conditions; this is your biggest chance for savings
Close unused rooms; do not heat or cool them	0	Depends on size of area closed off	If your kids are away at college, this savings will add up
During winter, open drapes and shades to let sun in; close at night to keep heat in; during summer, close drapes and shades to keep sun out	0	Can reduce heat grain up to 50%	Too many variables to give exact savings
Close damper in fireplace when fire is out	0	Impossible to measure	Closed flue keeps heat in and cold air out
Reduce hot water thermostat to 140° if you have a dishwasher; otherwise set it at 120°	0	$10 – $90	Savings depend on size of temperature reduction, cost of energy, and type of heater

continued on page 21

continued from page 20

Step	Cost	Annual Savings	Comments
Keep doors and windows closed as much as possible; turn off unneeded lights, TV, radio; open refrigerator and freezer as briefly as possible; dress appropriately for the season	0	Worthwhile but not quantifiable	Common sense goes a long way
Fill washer, dishwasher, avoiding partial loads; use warm wash and cold rinse on washer	0	$20 – $65	Depends on type of water heater and cost of energy
Take shower, not bath	0	$20 – $80	Bath consumes twice as much hot water
Avoid no-frost refrigerators	0	You'd save 40% by changing to manual model	Operating cost of frost-free model @ 3¢ per kilowatt hour: $50; manual: $30
Use oven to cook more than one dish at a time	0	Hard to calculate	
Turn off dishwasher when it reaches the dryng cycle	0	Small	Open door and let nature do the drying
Avoid TV sets with "instant-on" feature, or add a switch between set and the wall socket	0	Worthwhile	These sets have current running through some of their circuits even when the control knob is turned to "off"
On electric ranges, keep clean the reflector below heating element	0	Varies	Clean reflectors improve efficiency
Dry clothes in consecutive loads without interruption	0	Small	Once the dryer is heated, don't let it cool before you dry next load
Turn off dryer as soon as clothes are dry, or leave them damp for easier ironing	0	Varies	Some people let dryer run longer than necessary
Keep clean the dryer's lint screen	0	Small	Remove lint after each load
Use light colors on walls, carpets, furniture, and drapes	0	Considerable	Light colors reflect light, so you can use less illumination

continued on page 22

21

continued from page 21

Step	Cost	Annual Savings	Comments
Buy appliances on the basis of original cost **plus** operating expenses over the entire life of the appliance	0	Varies, but is likely to be substantial	An item with a higher first cost may be a better buy if its operating cost over, say, 10 years is low
In gas systems, turn off furnace's pilot and gas supply in warm weather	0	Worthwhile	For safety your gas company should do this
Turn up air-conditioner thermostat to 78°F or 80°F	0	Substantial	Each increase of 1° saves 3–5% of energy used by your air-conditioner
Reduce load on cooling system by cutting use of appliances during heat of day	0	Worthwhile	Appliances generate heat
Clean air-conditioner filter frequently	0	Worthwhile	This measure can bring 10% gain in efficiency
Cut out unnecessary and purely decorative lights	0	Varies	It takes ½ pint of oil to generate the electricity which a 100-watt floodlight uses to illuminate a garden for 10 hours
Avoid long-life lamps except in inaccessible places	0	Varies	Long-life lamps are less efficient

MODERATE COST MEASURES

Step	Cost	Annual Savings	Comments
Have heating system cleaned and adjusted every fall	$20–$40	10%	A dirty furnace wastes energy
Clean permanent furnace filter regularly; replace throw away filter every 60 days	Clean: 0 Replace: $2–$3	Hard to measure	If this chore is omitted for a long period, you'll pay for it
Install aluminum foil behind radiators	$1–$2	Hard to measure	This homemade reflector sends heat back into room
Weatherstrip doors and windows; caulk sills, seams, cracks, etc.	Depends on size of living unit	10% or more	Every break in the exterior lets cold in and heat out in winter; vice versa in summer

continued on page 23

continued from page 22

Step	Cost	Annual Savings	Comments
Fix leaky faucets, especially hot water faucets	Up to $25	$8–$35 a year	Leaks can waste 600–6,000 gallons of hot water a year
Shade your air-conditioner	Varies	Worthwhile	
Use kitchen, bathroom, and attic exhaust fans sparing	Small	Hard to measure	Fans expel heated air in winter and cooled air in summer
Make sure refrigerator and freezer gaskets are air-tight	New gasket costs up to $30	Up to 50% of operating costs	
Select a window air-conditioner which is properly sized and with a high **energy efficiency ratio**	Varies	Substantial	Ask dealer to let you consult Association of Home Appliance Manufacturers (AHAM) directory
Substitute fluorescent for incandescent lights where possible	Varies	75%	A 25-watt fluorescent has the light output of a 100-watt incandescent
Be sure damper in fireplace closes tightly; replace if necessary	$10–$50	Substantial	If damper doesn't work, much costly heat will go up chimney
Have your air-conditioner cleaned and lubricated during fall or winter	$20–$40 for each unit	If unit is dirty, savings will be substantial	Without cleaning, appliance loses 10–27% of efficiency; servicemen offer low rates in off-season
When buying new appliances, watch for energy-saving features (suds-saver, water saver on washing machines, power saver on ranges, etc.)	Energy savers raise cost of appliances only slightly	Small	Every little bit helps

MEASURES REQUIRING LARGER INITIAL INVESTMENT

Step	Cost	Annual Savings	Comments
In a central system, use air economizer which shuts down compressor and circulates outside air when it is cooler	$100 to $150	Will save 30% in Albany, 20% in Louisville, 37% in Portland, Ore.	This amounts to $27, $30, and $19, respectively, assuming a 2-ton unit and electricity @ 3¢ per kilowatt hour
Install storm windows and doors; use them in summer when pratical	$20 and up per window	$15%	You'll recover the cost in energy savings in a few years

continued on page 24

continued from page 23

Step	Cost	Annual Savings	Comments
If storm windows are too expensive, tape a sheet of plastic over each window	$5 per window	15%	If you rent, plastic may be your solution
Be sure you have recommended amount of insulation in attic, walls, and under floor. Consult the utility company for data in your area	Varies	20% or more (could be as much as 50%)	Keeps house warmer in winter, cooler in summer. You'll recover cost in a few years (sooner if you do your own installation)
Install awnings, sun screens, etc., to protect windows and doors from sun	Varies	Can cut solar heat gain up to 80%	Awnings should be designed so they won't trap hot air in window area
Plant appropriate shrubbery and trees around house	Varies	Substantial	Forms windscreen
Plant deciduous trees strategically	Varies	Substantial	They'll shade house in summer; allow sun to warm it in winter
Consider heat pump system, especially where entire house is heated and cooled by electricity	$2,000 to $4,000, depending on latitude and size of house	Varies, but can be substantial	Heat pump gives year-round climate conditioning, convenience, cleanliness
In a centralized **cooling** and heating system, insulate ducts at least 1½"	Cost varies with size— $200 or more	As much as 25%	This is especially important if ducts run through uninsulated attics

HIRING A CONTRACTOR

Most energy conservation work can be done by the do-it-yourselfer. Yet there are some jobs you will want to leave to the professional. Since many firms in the energy saving business are relatively new, it pays to pick a contractor carefully. New fields are notorious for spawning fly-by-nighters who prey on the uninformed.

The best way to pick a contractor may be to get the name from a friend or relative who has had similar work done and was satisfied with the results. Another way to get a good one is to ask another tradesman who has done good work for you. It is unlikely that he will give you the name of someone who does questionable work.

If you can't get a direct recommendation, you can start by checking the Yellow Pages, or inquiring at your local Chamber of Commerce. Or, if possible, consult the local agencies who run government-funded or non-profit home improvement programs.

Compile a list of three or four contractors (it doesn't matter whether the contractor is a one-man operation or a large company) and give each a schedule of the work you want done. If the job is going to amount to more than $200, get written estimates and names of past customers. Check out each contractor's references. Call your banker or local credit bureau agent to learn which contractors are reliable. And, finally, determine how long each contractor has been in business. Usually, the longer the better.

GET A CONTRACT

Even if you are hiring a man directly recommended by your mother, get a contract. It should be detailed, showing all materials to be used, and exactly what is to be done. If there is a warranty for the job, find out exactly what this means, and the cost. The warranty should specify when payment is due.

Generally, it's best to pay as you go, making the final payment a week or two after the job is complete. If some portion of the project should fail, the contractor will want to correct the situation so he can get paid. Also, get written confirmation of the contractor's liability coverage. If one of the workmen gets hurt on the job, you don't want to have to be financially responsible for the consequences.

Taking these precautions does not necessarily mean that you distrust the contractor. But a written, specific contract can avoid any misunderstanding.

Chapter 2
How to Use Insulation Effectively

How to Use Insulation Effectively

Installing insulation in your home is probably the single most important thing you can do to cut energy costs. Not everyone, of course, will be able to insulate the entire house at once, and every area of the home may not require insulation. However, if you are starting from scratch, the attic should be the first phase of the project. Next insulate your home's basement or crawlspace. Most difficult to insulate effectively are the exterior walls.

TYPES OF INSULATION

Insulation is available in a variety of types, most of which can be installed relatively easily by the do-it-yourselfer. Insulation comes in four basic forms: flexible, loose-fill, rigid boards and foamed-in-place. Materials used include mineral wool, cellulose fiber, vermiculite, perlite, reflective foil and plastic foams (polyrethane, polystyrene and urea formaldehyde). Mineral wool, either fiberglass or rock wool, is the most widely used type. It's available in flexible batts, blankets, and loose-fill (poured or blown into place).

Batts are pre-cut in lengths of 4' and 8'. Blankets come in rolls. Rolls made by different companies come in varying lengths, but generally will be around 40'. Batts and blankets are most often used in unfinished attics, between basement and crawlspace joists, and in walls that are still under construction. The material is installed between framing members of new houses or when new rooms are being added to old houses.

Batts and blankets have the same characteristics:

1. They are cut 15″ or 23″ wide to fit snugly between joists, rafters and studs that are constructed on 16-inch or 24-inch centers.
2. They come in thicknesses of 1–12 inches.
3. They come with or without a vapor barrier. A vapor barrier helps prevent water vapor from condensing and collecting on rafters, joists, and studs. Vapor barriers attached to batts and blankets are made of asphalt or aluminum foil.

LOOSE-FILL INSULATION

Do-it-yourself loose-fill insulation is poured into place. It is ideal for attics which have obstructions between beams. With loose fill, you avoid the cutting and fitting necessary with blankets or batts. Before you pour loose fill into an attic, you may need to install a vapor barrier, as explained later.

Special pneumatic equipment is needed for loose-fill insulation that is blown into place. A hole is made in a wall or floor if access is not possible any other way. The material is blown in and the hole access closed off.

Loose-fill insulation of the poured and blown-in variety is manufactured from various materials. Cellulose fiber is made from newspaper, wood filter, and other organic materials. It consists of smaller tufts than mineral wool, another type, and more consistently gets into small nooks and corners.

Cellulose fiber resists fire and vermin, if properly treated, but it is not moisture resistant, and high attic temperatures may vaporize its fire-retardant chemicals. On the other hand, cellulose has greater resistance to heat passing through it (on an "R" per inch basis) than mineral wool or fiberglass. This can be important if you don't have much space for insulation. Of the two types of cellulose, Class I is better than Class II.

Vermiculite, another type of loose fill, has only about 70% of the heat resistant value of fiberglass or mineral wool. On the other hand, vermiculite pours readily and is commonly used to insulate masonry blocks.

If you decide to use cellulose fiber insulation, make certain the bags state that the material meets the latest federal specifications, HH-1-515C (4/13/76), which establish minimum thermal qualities for cellulosic or wood fiber insulation.

FOAM-IN-PLACE INSULATION

Foam (or urea formaldehyde) insulation must be applied by a contractor. It is used primarily to insulate finished walls. Since this type of insulation is relatively new, it pays to choose qualified contractors who use material from established firms and who will guarantee their work.

At this point in time, foam insulation is recommended for exterior side walls, block or core insulation only. It is not recommended for attics and cathedral ceilings. Foam insulation requires an almost air-tight, relatively inert atmosphere for long-term effectiveness.

Manufacturers report that there is no problem in using foam where fiberglass insulation is already present. They say there is zero chemical reaction between the two materials and, since foam insulation is applied under pressure, it readily compresses and flows around any existing insulation in the wall.

Borden Chemical's Insulspray foam system, for example, is comprised of a urea-formaldehyde resin, a catalyst or foaming agent, mixed in a gun activated by compressed air. The foam sets up in about 20 minutes, but continues drying for 24 to 48 hours. Evaporation of volatile ingredients, according to the company, does give off a faint but harmless odor. Standard procedure is to leave the exterior wall "open" for two days, and to raise the windows slightly if an odor is noticed. The experiences is said to be no more traumatic than paint in a house.

RIGID BOARD INSULATION

Rigid board insulation is commonly used for basement walls, the perimeter insulation of floor slabs, and in new construction. In many cases, it can be installed when siding is being replaced.

There are various types of rigid board insulation: polystyrene, urethane, glass fiber, and bead board. The first two may not require a vapor barrier; bead board and glass fiber do. All types of rigid board insulation must meet the requirements of local fire codes. This usually means covering the rigid board with gypsum board. Some rigid board insulation comes with a gypsum board covering.

R VALUES AND LABELS

When figuring how much insulation you should install, forget inches. R value is a more accurate means of designating the performance of insulation. R stands for resistance to winter heat loss and summer heat gain. Even though two brands of insulation may be of different thicknesses, if they are rated at the same R value, they will perform the same.

Never buy a brand of insulation that is not plainly marked with the R value, and only talk to a contractor in R value terms. For comparison, you can use Fig. 2-1 to determine the approximate relationships between R value and inches.

Adding two pieces of insulation together provides an R value that is the sum total of the individual R values. Thus, an insulation batt rated at R-19 placed together with another insulation batt rated at R-19 will provide a total R value of R-38.

With loose-fill insulation, federal specifications require that each bag of mineral wool and cellulose fiber carry a label. The following is an example label to give you an idea of what it looks like and what it means:

R value	Minimum thickness	Maximum net coverage per bag
R-30	13¾"	33 sq. ft.
R-22	10"	45 sq. ft.
R-11	5"	90 sq. ft.

The label can help you establish how many bags of loose-fill insulation you or a contractor will need to achieve the desired R value. Here is how it is done:

1. Multiply the overall square foot area of your attic floor or exterior walls by .90 or .94. The constant .90 is used if joists or studs are 16" apart. The constant .94 is used if joists or studs are 24" apart.

2. Divide the result by the "maximum net coverage per bag" given on the label for the R value you desire. The result is the number of bags.

TYPICAL R VALUES OF VARIOUS INSULATION TYPES

	R/INCH	INCHES NEEDED FOR					
		R11	R19	R22	R34	R38	R49
LOOSE FILL BLOWN-MACHINE FIBERGLASS	R2.25	5	8.5	10	15.5	17	22
MINERAL WOOL	R3.135	3.5	6	7	11	12.5	16
CELLULOSE	R3.7	3	5.5	6	9.5	10.5	13.5
LOOSE FILL POURED-HAND CELLULOSE	R3.7	3	5.5	6	9.5	10.5	13.5
MINERAL WOOL	R3.125	3.5	6	7	11	12.5	16
FIBERGLASS	R2.25	5	8.5	10	15.5	17	22
VERMICULITE	R2.1	5.5	9	10.5	16.5	18	23.5
BATTS OR BLANKETS FIBERGLASS	R3.14	3.5	6	7	11	12.5	16
MINERAL WOOL	R3.14	3.5	6	7	11	12.5	16
RIGID BOARD POLYSTYRENE BEADBOARD	R3.6	3	5.5	6.5	9.5	10.5	14
EXTRUDED POLYSTYRENE (STYROFOAM)	R4-5.41	3-2	5-3.5	5.5-4	8.5-6.5	9.5-7	12.5-9
URETHANE	R6.2	2	3	3.5	5.5	6.5	8
FIBERGLASS	R4.0	3	5	5.5	8.5	9.5	12.5
FOAM UREAFORMALDEHYDE	R4.8 (35°F)	2.5	4	4.5	7	8	10.5

Fig. 2-1. A comparison of the relationship between R value and inches according to the insulation type. Source: Minnesota Energy Agency.

For example, if the overall square footage of your attic floor is 640, joists are 16″ apart, you want an R value of 30, and each bag covers 33 sq. ft., then 640 × .90 = 576 ÷ 33 = 18 bags.

The Federal Housing Administration has established a minimum standard for new homes of R-19 or R-22 in attics (depending on climate), R-11 in basements and crawlspaces, R-11 or R-13 in walls (depending on climate). For the most part, manufacturers such as Owens-Corning (Fig. 2-2) suggest higher values, and the recommendation has merit.

To calculate how many square (not running) feet of insulation you need, do the following:

1. Calculate the overall area to be covered (length × width).
2. If joists, rafters or studs are 16″ apart, multiply by .90. If joists or studs are 24″ apart, multiply by .94. This gives the number of square feet of insulation you will need.

For example, if the overall area to be covered is 640 sq. ft., and joists are 16″ apart, then 640 × .90 = 576 sq. ft. of insulation.

32

TIPS ON INSTALLING

The actual job of installing insulation is easily done by a homeowner. Following is a list of the equipment you'll need.

- A utility knife, heavy shears or a serrated-edge kitchen knife to cut batts and blankets. The latter works as well as anything else.
- A straightedge for a cutting guide. A rigid metal ruler or short length of board will work.
- A measuring tape.
- A rake or similar tool to push or pull blankets and batts to eave edges in attics if there isn't sufficient headroom.
- Boards to walk on in an unfinished attic so you won't plunge your foot through the ceiling below. A few pieces of ¾" utility grade plywood 4' long and 12" to 16" wide will do nicely.
- Some sort of light. A mechanic's trouble light is suitable, as well as a clamp-on photo lamp.
- A staple gun.

Remember, barriers face the warm-in-winter side.

Batts and blankets have flanges. They provide a sturdy base for stapling the blanket or batt to wood framing. It's not necessary to staple material to framing if the batt or blanket is laid flat, as it would be when insulating the attic floor. If an area is narrower than the width of the blanket or batt, cut only the insulation—not the flanges and/or vapor barrier—to the exact width.

It is imporant that you leave no voids when installing insulation. Every gap should be filled. Butt the ends of blankets or batts tightly together or cut back the insulation about 2" at one end of the blanket or batt. Then join the material together, lapping the vapor barrier of the cut blanket or batt over the other.

Cut small, separate pieces of insulation and place them into small or irregular areas, such as around pipes that pass through the attic floor, and in cracks around window frames in a newly built room. Do not compress insulation. Let if fall into place naturally. Compression reduces the insulating properties of the material.

If you can't get blanket or batt material into a place, fill the area with loose-fill insulation. However, remember that it is best to install a vapor barrier. In the case of loose fill (plus batts or blankets not

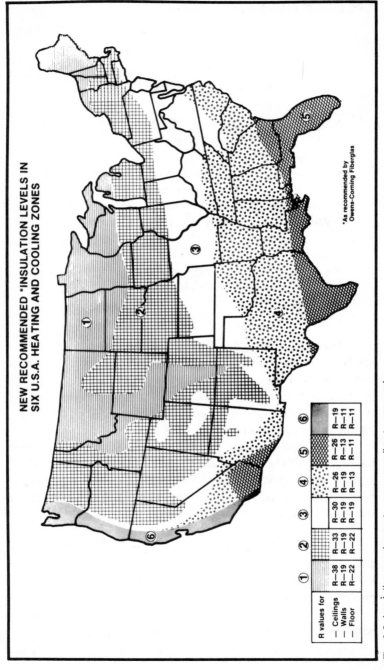

NEW RECOMMENDED *INSULATION LEVELS IN SIX U.S.A. HEATING AND COOLING ZONES

R values for	①	②	③	④	⑤	⑥
— Ceilings	R—38	R—33	R—30	R—26	R—26	R—19
— Walls	R—19	R—19	R—19	R—19	R—13	R—11
— Floor	R—22	R—22	R—19	R—13	R—11	R—11

*As recommended by
Owens-Corning Fiberglas

Fig. 2-2. Insulation requirements vary according to geography.

outfitted with a vapor barrier), staple 2 mil or thicker polyethylene sheeting to sidewalls. Remember that the vapor barrier faces the warm side.

Where insulation batts or blankets have to be secured along basement joists and between wall studs, drive ½" staples at the ends of the batts or blankets along the length of the flanges. Space the staples 6" apart.

If you should accidentally tear the vapor barrier, cover it with a piece of vapor barrier from a scrap section of batt or blanket, taping it down. Or cut a piece of polyethylene sheeting to size and tape this over the torn section.

INSULATION IN ATTICS

If your attic is completely unfinished, insulate the floor (Fig. series 2-3 through 2-7). There is no need to also insulate between rafters. If the attic is completed and insulation is required, blow-in equipment will be needed.

Note that if you plan to finish an attic for living quarters, do not insulate between floor joists; this would prevent you from benefitting from heat that rises from the lower floor.

It is very important that adequate ventilation is maintained to allow hot air in summer and moisture in winter to escape. Pros recommend 1 sq. ft. of net free vent area for every 150 to 300 sq. ft. of attic floor area, depending on your specific conditions. Also, when you insulate an attic, make sure eave vents are not covered.

When installing batts or blankets, take special care that the material doesn't cover vent plates. If you are using loose fill, construct a wooden or cardboard baffle (or lay pieces of thick batts next to vents) so insulation won't block the flow of air from vents into the attic. This will also keep wind from disturbing the loose wool.

Before you install insulation, check the attic for water leaks. Insulation loses its effectiveness when wet.

To insulate an attic floor where there is not now insulation, lay batts or blankets between beams. Slide insulation under wiring where possible. You do not have to staple the material in place. Remember to face the vapor barrier down. If the batt or blanket has no vapor barrier, first staple in polyethylene material, either sealing seams with tape or overlapping ends 6".

Fig. 2-3. Before buying your insulation, measure the joists on your attic floor. You can buy insulation in either 16 or 24″ widths to fit snugly between the beams.

Be sure all nooks are filled, but leave a 3″ space around recessed lighting fixtures or exhaust fans. When using cellulose some pros first cover recessed light fixtures with asbestos. The space between the chimney and wood framing should be filled with a material that is non-combustible.

Fig. 2-4. Be sure to open packages only when and where you plan to use them. Fiberglass insulation will expand to many times its packaged size, when the bag is opened.

To fit batts or blankets snugly around cross bracing, cut the ends. Then, cut the end to the adjoining batt in a similar way to allow ends to butt tightly together.

Note that if you are adding insulation batts or blankets on top of existing insulation, the new insulation should not have a vapor barrier. Buy unfaced material. If it is not available, and you have to use batts or blankets having a vapor barrier, remove the barrier or slash it freely with a knife. Install the material with the slashed surface down.

For unheated crawlspace areas, insert batts or blankets between floor joists from below and secure with chicken wire or other restrainer. This may be chicken wire that is stapled to framing or wire that you tie between nails. In this case the vapor barrier faces up.

Fig. 2-5. Cut batts of insulation to fit around obstructions in attic. An ordinary, serrated bread knife works. Be sure you wear gloves and long sleeves.

Fig. 2-6. Where headroom is lacking in attics, one way to do the job is to use a wax applicator, mop or broom handle to push the insulation into place.

INSULATING WALLS YOURSELF

It may be possible to insulate finished walls yourself. Go into the attic and check around the perimeter. Is studding open? If so, shine a flashlight down between the studs to be certain there are no obstructions. If not, one option is to pour vermiculite or perlite down the wall between studs. A better option, especially if wall studs aren't ex-

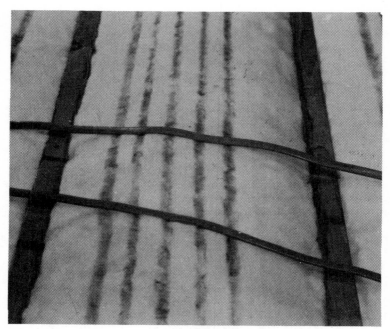

Fig. 2-7. When installing insulation in the attic, place it carefully under wires.

Fig. 2-8. If walls are not open, insulation will have to be blown in by a professional.

Fig. 2-9. Batts and blankets are used for walls under construction. Batts are pre-cut to 4' to 8', while blankets come in rolls of about 40'.

posed or aren't accessible, or if there are obstructions in the wall, is to call a contractor to blow or gun-in insulation (Fig. 2-8).

In a newly constructed room, fit the end of the blanket or batt snugly against the top of the framing. Working down, staple the flanges to the sides of the studs. With aluminum foil-faced blankets, staple the material so an air space is left. Cut the blanket to fit tightly against the framing at the bottom. If more than one piece of material is used in the same stud space, butt the ends tightly together.

For basements, you can buy special unfaced masonry wall blanket insulation (used with polyethylene sheeting as a vapor barrier), foam boards (covered with gypsum board), or if your walls are rough, you can have a contractor "trowel on" foam (Fig. series 2-9 through 2-12). Important: If you live in far northern areas, check your plans with local experts to avoid eventual frost heaving in the foundation.

WHERE ELSE TO INSULATE

In addition to conventional insulation jobs, other insulating opportunities exist within your home. One such is the water heater.

Kits to insulate water heaters are available commercially; you do the job with standard blankets of insulation. Cut for fit around the circumference of the heater and for length from top to bottom. Leave openings for faucet drain, plates, vents, controls, and access to gas burner. You can insulate the top of electric heater tanks, but not gas heaters.

Also consider insulating heating ducts and water pipes. If your water heater, ducts or water pipes are in unheated spaces, there's no question you'll save energy dollars. Even if your basement is finished off it will pay. While heat radiating from the water heater, ducts or pipes is not "lost" during the heating season, this heat will drive up your cooling bills in summer.

Insulate pipes which pass through walls (if you're building or remodeling and pipes are accessible) or through any unheated space. The same is true of heating ducts or pipes passing through attics.

Other locations to insulate: If you have radiant (baseboard) hot water heat, insulate the loops which connect the panels from room to room. You will find on the basement side that these feeder-pipes are

Fig. 2-10. In new construction, fit insulation against top of framing and work down, stapling flanges to the sides of the studs.

2' to 10' long and more. Their temperature is 180°F (as opposed to hot water piping, which is 120°F to 140°F). Also consider insulating cold water pipes in the basement. Insulation will prevent moisture from condensing and dripping on the floor when humid summer air encounters cold basement pipes.

Insulation can also be used as a sound deadener to reduce motor noises of your furnace. In this case, line the motor compartment and wrap the ducts (first having nailed them to ceiling joists).

Special duct and pipe insulation is available at many hardware stores, lumberyards, and home care centers. If not, all-purpose fiberglass insulation can be used. On heating ducts, cut to fit with overlap, then wrap and wire insulation firmly to duct. On hot or cold water pipes, cut the insulation in strips, wrap spirally and cement the ends down.

SAFETY PRECAUTIONS

While installing insulation is not a hazardous job, you should take some precautions to protect yourself.

Fig. 2-11. Cut blankets to fit against frame at bottom. If more than one piece of blanket is used in the same stud space, butt the ends snugly together.

Fig. 2-12. Cut separate pieces of insulation for small or irregular areas, such as around window frames. Don't compress the material too much lest you destroy the insulating property of the material.

If fiberglass insulation is being installed, wear protective gear to guard against irritation from fibers. Wear a loose-fitting long-sleeved shirt and trousers, as well as gloves and a face mask. A simple paper breathing mask is fine. If you wear glasses, a mask with a rigid plastic is good. These masks fit over the eyes and reduce eyeglass "fogging." Other suggestions worth considering:

- Use adequate light. A trouble light (bulb in wire cage) or a spotlight that can be clamped to framing member is good. Keep the light away from the insulation.
- Don't smoke in the attic. While insulation is not likely to catch fire, the attic is a dry place.
- When working in the attic, be wary of nails protruding through the roofing.
- For comfort when doing an attic or crawlspace, wear mason's or gardener's pads or ordinary basketball pads on the knees.

Chapter 3
What You Can Do
about Doors and Windows

What You Can Do about Doors and Windows

There are a number of ways you can cut down on the loss of energy through conventional windows and doors. The most common way is to install storm windows and storm doors; these provide dead air space which inhibits heat convection. In general, you can expect to reduce heat loss by 50% with storm windows and doors.

BUYING STORM WINDOWS

Storm windows are made of various materials, but there's really no need to consider anything other than aluminum. Aluminum storm windows are available in three finishes: mill, anodized and baked enamel. On the low end of the quality scale is mill. This is really just raw aluminum, unpainted and untreated. Mill has a tendency to pit and corrode even if you paint it. This malady can lead to windows that are difficult to operate.

Anodized aluminum is metal that has been chemically treated for weather protection. However, the best finish is baked enamel. Baked enamel windows are durable, highly resistant to scratching, and come in a variety of colors.

There are ways you can determine the quality of window construction. First check the thickness (or gauge) of the aluminum. The thicker the better. Heavier gauge aluminum will keep its shape longer and retain its fasteners, such as screws, longer.

Check the corners. Every storm window frame has two vertical and two horizontal members. Corners on some windows are mitered, while butt joints are used on others. The better miter joints will have reinforcing pieces. In either case (butt or miter), a good joint has its members fitting together tightly. If these joints separate, leaks can develop and render the window less energy efficient.

Check the interlock or the vinyl or rubber strip between window panels. The interlock must provide snug sealing.

The insert can be another indicator of quality. Also made of vinyl or rubber, it is used to seal one side of the glass. It should be 5/16" or 3/8" thick. For even better quality, you can get panels with so-called marine sealing: vinyl inserts all around the glass.

Storm windows should have safety glass. If you store them in the summer, safety glass will help protect against breakage. More important, if safety glass is broken, it will fracture into blunt- (rather than sharp-) edged pieces. You can also get storm windows with panes made of acrylic sheeting instead of glass.

Prices on standard storm windows, you will discover, vary greatly. Low quality storm windows will retail for one third the price of high quality units.

When buying storm doors and windows, you should be aware of the importance of A.I.R. Those letters represent the air infiltration rate of a door or window unit. In the storm door/window industry, you may find units that allow as much as 4 cfm (cubic feet per minute) of air infiltration. However, better units keep air infiltration rates as low as .05 cfm.

REPLACING STORM DOORS

Quality makes a difference with storm doors as well. Here are suggestions from experts to keep in mind when you start shopping around.

- Thickness of a good door is between 7/8" and 1"; a better door averages 1 1/4".
- The kickplate should be reinforced with metal.
- The door should not open more than 90 degrees and should have a chain, a good pneumatic cylinder and a built-in lock.
- A good door will have a protective grillwork over the bottom glass.
- Panes should be made of safety glass or acrylic sheeting.

To replace your storm door, remove the hinges of the old door, if it's wood, or remove the screws spaced around the frame, if it's metal. Disconnect the door closer and retaining chain.

Most replacement storm doors are manufactured with the frame and door locked together with clips to hold the unit square until it's placed in the frame. Do not remove the clips until the door is installed. There will be extra length on the bottom of the door rails. Measuring from the top of the frame, cut off the bottom of the rails with a hacksaw (Fig. 3-1). Cut only enough to slide the unit easily into the door frame. Now set the storm unit in the frame, check the side rail with a level to be sure the unit is sitting plumb in the opening (Fig. 3-2), and screw the unit into place (Fig. 3-3).

When the door is secured in the wood frame, remove the clips which hold door and siderails together. Now open the door to apply the lockset. The lockset consists of the outside handle and push-button, the inside handle and lock, and a metal rod which is the plunger that moves the lock mechanism from the outside. Because the height of the lockset may vary, storm doors often come without pre-drilled holes for lock placement. Make sure the lockset on the storm door does not interfere with the door knob of the main door.

You can use the old storm door for a guide in placing the lock on the new storm door. Setting the lock back about ¾″ from the door

Fig. 3-1. Measure height of existing door frame. Cut away excess length on storm door frame with a hacksaw.

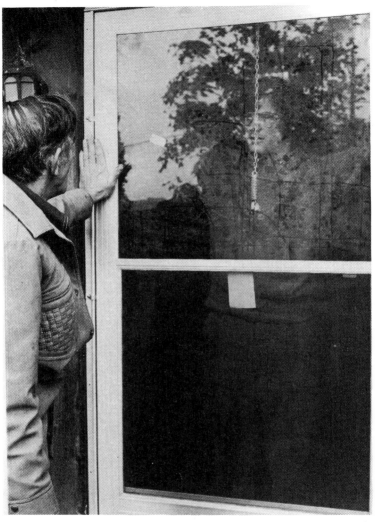

Fig. 3-2. Set storm door in opening. Do not remove metal retaining clips on right side of door until frame is secured to wood jamb.

edge, and at a height so it won't bump against the exterior door knob, drill three ¼" holes. Use the interior handle base for a template and drill a pilot hole of ⅛" through the screw holes in the inside handle (Fig. 3-4). Then drill out these two holes through with the ¼" bit, passing completely through the door. Measure the center between these two holes, and bore a ¼" hole here for the metal rod, or plunger. You may have to ream this center hole to ⅜″ to allow the plunger to move freely.

Oil the moving parts of the lock. Then fit the plunger in the outside part. Place the inside part so that the plunger fits into the slot, and secure the outer and inner pieces in place with screws.

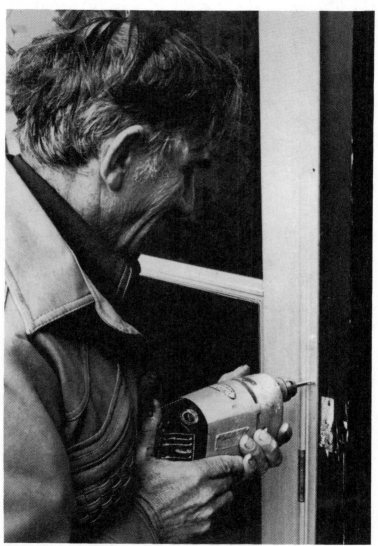

Fig. 3-3. Attach frame with screws at pre-drilled holes. Use variable speed drill. A Phillips bit will speed work.

Fig. 3-4. Drill three ¼" holes through door to secure lock. Use the inside portion of the lock for a template to locate the holes.

Position the door catch on the wooden frame so that the latch strikes it in the middle. A shim is supplied to go under the catch, or strike plate, to adjust the catch (Fig. 3-5). Close the door, and adjust the position of the door catch until the door latches properly. Then tighten the screws that hold the catch.

Now install the door closer. Allow the door to swing shut naturally a couple of times. Then adjust by turning the cylinder at the plunger end of the closer and by re-positioning the plunger in the notch on the storm door bracket.

Use the retainer chain assembly to prevent the wind from slamming the door off the hinges (Fig. 3-6). Slight adjustment may be necessary to be sure that door handle, latch, closer retaining chain and weatherstripping are all properly placed.

The final step is to insure a good fit at the bottom of the door. Some units have an adjustable bar that may be lowered by loosening screws. The unit shown has two metal door shoes with rubber gaskets attached. Cut these for length, allowing the rubber to slightly overlap the corners of the door. Set the rubber against the wooden sill and drill screw holes at the bottom of the slots in the metal strip. Push the shoes down to insure a good seal between rubber and door sill. Tighten the screws to hold the shoes in place.

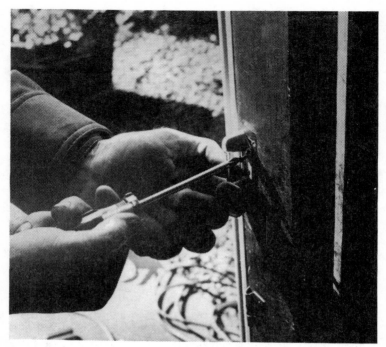

Fig. 3-5. Set door latch on wood door jamb to match lock height on storm door. An extra spacer, if needed, can be found under the latch.

Fig. 3-6. Install door closer, retaining chain and spring so they're in this position when door is open. Chain protects door from wind damage.

Fig. 3-7. Remove inside molding, plus cords and weights or spring balances, and take out old wood sash.

HOW TO UPDATE WINDOWS

If you have double glazed windows, or regular windows with storms, another way to convert double glazed windows, or conventional windows with storms, is by adding a plastic storm window from inside the house. These are available in kit form in many hardware stores. They use plastic frames that can be cut to size and fitted around a sheet of clear acrylic plastic. Some have a pressure sensitive adhesive on the back of the frame. After removing the

53

protective paper, the unit is pressed against the molding around the house window. This seals the window for the winter.

One company in the business of making inside plastic storm windows estimates that these units will save the homeowner 6% of his fuel costs, provided the house is well insulated, has storm windows and tightly weatherstripped windows.

If you're planning to improve your present home, you can install windows with double-pane insulating glass. One window manufacturer notes that quality windows with double-pane insulating glass can provide the same insulating benefits as a tight-fitting storm sash

Fig. 3-8. Pry out parting stops at top and sides to allow top sash to be taken out.

Fig. 3-9. All sashes in new windows are taken out for easy handling of the frame.

over single-glazed windows. Window manufacturers have developed new and more efficient weatherstripping systems which greatly reduce heat loss compared to loose-fitting windows, new or old.

Replacing an existing window with new conventional windows can be a rather involved job. However there are a number of companies now making windows designed for easier installation. Typically, these windows are ordered to the exact size needed. They don't require modification of the wall, only removal of the old sashes (window panels). The old framing stays in the wall. The photo sequence (Figs. 3-7 through 3-12) gives an idea of the procedure.

If you are replacing windows and have a choice, position them to take advantage of solar heat. To get more sun, position windows, especially large windows, facing south. The Department of Energy points out that solar heat gained from a large window can exceed that window's total conductive heat loss during the day. Windows facing east and west enjoy the sun's rays only part of the day, while those facing north get little or no sun and should be the smallest.

REPLACING EXTERIOR DOORS

Exterior doors that are either in bad shape or are not energy efficient should be replaced. Normally, this is a difficult job. But here, too, manufacturers have come up with doors that are not only easier to install, but specially designed to cut energy losses.

Fig. 3-10. With header expander in place, new frame is positioned and shimmed for square fit.

Fig. 3-11. Window is removed, then blind stops are caulked at both top and sides.

Insulated doors of metal instead of wood, say the manufacturers, provide insulation and weatherstripping that stop from 2½ to 6 times more energy loss than conventional wood entrances. Storm doors can be added to cut energy losses even further, but in most cases won't be needed. Insulated metal doors are generally filled with a high density polyurethane foam. This, according to manufacturers, forms an insulating "sandwich" with more heat-blocking values than an ordinary door/storm door combination.

Insulated doors can be ordered with hinges on either edge for right or left hand swing. Step-by-step drawings and full instructions for installing are included with each unit. One company's steel door installation involves just three main steps:

1. Remove the old door, inside trim, threshold and hardware.
2. Nail replacement unit into place and attach anchor screws.

3. Apply pre-weatherstripped wood stops and fasten and caulk sill.

Insulated doors come prehung, complete with door, frame and threshold, all fully weathersealed. The replacement job shown in the photos (Figs. 3-13 through 3-18) can be completed in 2½ hours. Besides saving on energy costs, the doors also offer the security and the maintenance-free qualities of steel.

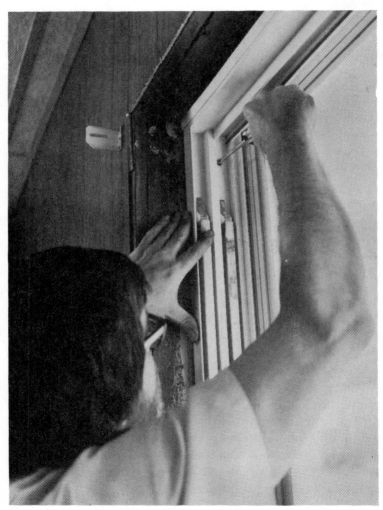

Fig. 3-12. New frame is fastened with screws, fitted with both sashes. Then caulk front, attach expander header and replace inside stops.

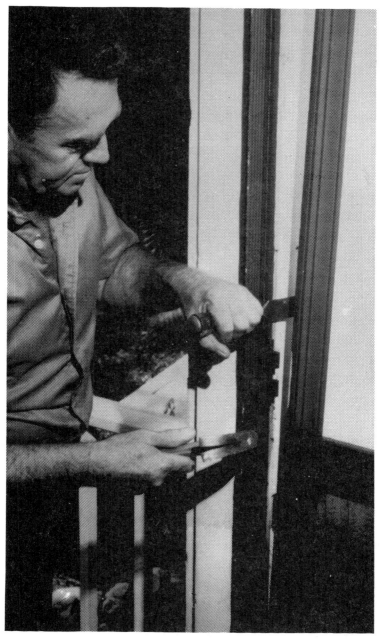

Fig. 3-13. Remove old door, strip off outside casings, and remove interior casings.

Fig. 3-14. Remove old sill and jambs; position door in frame.

Fig. 3-15. Shim inside between jambs and studs for even spacing.

Fig. 3-16. Check with level to make sure that frame is plumb.

Fig. 3-17. Nail in jambs; screw through top hinge and jamb into studs.

Fig. 3-18. Caulk around molding, install lock, and paint.

Newer styles of insulated doors feature traditional and modern designs, deep-embossed into the steel on both sides of the door to create the look of paneling. Other models offer a variety of choices with insulated glass as an option. The doors are available as single or double doors in standard sizes, and are electrostatically primed with an acrylic enamel paint.

Chapter 4
How to Use Caulking
and Weatherstripping

There's no doubt that if you saw a 4" or 5" square hole in the side of your heated or air-conditioned home, you would patch it quickly. The fact is that all the openings around windows and doors of many homes would add up to a hole of that size or larger. Collectively, these narrow little openings amount to one large energy-wasting opening.

CAULKING

Sealing openings with caulking and weatherstripping is one of the easiest and most economical ways to save home energy. The time to caulk is during the warmer months of spring, summer and early fall, before temperatures turn cold. Below 40°F. caulk may not cure properly and condensation of moisture can prevent a solid bond.

Where to begin? Air openings are usually found where different types of materials are joined, or where material is simply cracked or broken. For example, look for openings between masonry and wood or metal door and window frames, between walls and woodwork or baseboards and around pipes.

Several different types of caulks are available from a number of manufacturers. In the long run it will pay to base your selection of caulking compound on its performance characteristics compared to requirements of the job, not on purchase price alone. To find out the best type of caulk to use in your specific case, consult a reputable

Fig. 4-1. Silicone rubber caulk and sealer forms a permanently flexible and waterproof seal around windows and doors. Source: Dow-Corning.

paint, hardware or building supply dealer. Generally, one of the synthetic, flexible or water-base caulk products (Fig. 4-1) will best serve the needs of most homeowners.

Butyl rubber caulk, for example, will provide maximum exterior durability, with exceptional resistance to shock, heat and cold. Acrylic latex caulk is the easiest of all caulk to use, offering almost unlimited application, both indoors and out. The bead can be smoothed with a wet finger, clean-up is fast with water, and it can be painted immediately with any of the latex paints. Oil base caulking is the most inexpensive, but tends to harden as it dries out, becoming more vulnerable to crumbling than other types.

When caulking an air leak, make sure the surface is properly prepared. This will help to assure a tight seal when the caulk is applied. Use a putty knife and brush to clear away any loose material from the crack to be sealed, and remove any oil or grease with mineral spirits. Keep in mind, too, that unpainted metal surfaces should be primed to prevent rust.

Usually it's best not to caulk a crack more than ¼" wide or ¼" deep. For deep cracks, pack the crevice with oakum (available at paint, hardware and plumbing supply stores) to within ¼" of the surface before caulking.

Although many caulks are available in "toothpaste type" tubes, best results are usually achieved with cartridge-caulk, applied with a caulking gun. The cartridge is held by an arm or barrel, and a trigger operated plunger forces caulk through a tapered nozzle into the crack to be filled. Open the cartridge by slicing off the tip of the nozzle, but remember that the width of the bead is determined by the location of the cut—near the tip for a narrow bead, and closer to the cartridge itself for a wider bead. Be sure to cut the tip at an angle, too.

Fig. 4-2. Old weatherstripping is easily removed from door jamb with screwdriver and small pliers.

Fig. 4-3. Miter weatherstripping at corners where top and side meet.

Smooth, steady pressure on the trigger will give you an even bead. Any excess or uneven caulk can be smoothed with a fingertip or small trowel, wetted with water or mineral spirits (check manufacturer's directions), depending on the type of caulk being used.

Fig. 4-4. Metal weatherstripping is nailed to door frame, using small brads supplied with the purchase.

Finally, seal the tip of the cartridge with masking tape when the job is completed. This will help to keep the caulk soft enough for gunning the next time you see a need for on- the-spot home insulation.

WEATHERSTRIPPING

Weatherstripping windows and doors prevents heat loss around loose frames (Figs. 4-2 through 4-5). If you find moisture or

Fig. 4-5. Narrow metal strip is provided to fit behind door latch and inside wider strips.

Fig. 4-6. To use adhesive-backed foam, you just strip off protective paper and lay it in place.

ice on the inner surfaces of the storm windows in cold weather, you know the windows are loose and permit warm air from the inside of your home to pass through and condense moisture on the cold surface of the storm window. The solution is to weatherstrip.

A great variety of weatherstrip material is available at hardware and home center stores and installation is usually easy. You can use ¼″ self-sticking sponge rubber or urethane foam (Fig. 4-6) stripping on the underside of the lower sash and on the top of the upper sash. You can also place spring bronze or aluminum stripping in the same places. Caulking may be used around doors and windows (Figs. 4-7 and 4-8).

Fig. 4-7. Roll caulking is pressed into cracks around doors and windows.

For the sides of double hung sliding windows, wool felt stripping reinforced with notched zinc is efficient and durable. It's easily fastened in place with small nails in a vertical position next to the sash (Fig. 4-9). If you don't like the appearance of the stripping at the

Fig. 4-8. Here roll caulking is used to seal cracks in exterior of storm windows. Just unroll, press into place.

Fig. 4-9. Weatherstrip sheathed in serrated metal is installed with nails. It is not particularly pretty but it is permanent.

front of the window, you can mount it behind the lower sash on the parting bead and behind the upper sash on the outermost wood strip or blind stop.

Another type of weatherstripping you can use along the sides of windows is made of hair felt and attached with small nails or staples. By far the oldest and least expensive stripping, hair felt is highly effective but less popular than other types because of its conspicuous color and rough appearance. However, it can be mounted behind the upper and lower sashes on the parting and outside beads which form the tracks in which the sashes move.

The ¼" wide urethane foam stripping mentioned above can also be used around windows, including the sill on the inside. Since it is narrow and either white or very pale gray, it is quite inconspicuous. Plastic foams are much more effective in retaining heat and stopping drafts if they are of the "closed cell" type.

You can also seal up certain windows in the house for the cold weather season. An easy way is to use self-sticking 1″ wide clear polyethylene tape (Fig. 4-10) on the sash frame and the trim next to it so that the tape covers the crack between them. The crack at the meeting rails should also be covered to effectively shut out all drafts. The tape can be easily removed. Another way to seal windows for the winter is to use a soft putty-like material in all the cracks around the window.

Exterior doors can account for big heat losses. To reduce energy waste you can use aluminum stripping with a tubular vinyl insert along one side. Mount the stripping on the door stops so that the closed door will compress the soft vinyl tube and form a tight seal. Another type of door weatherstripping is made of wood about ⅜″ thick and 1″ wide with a soft plastic foam down one edge of the

Fig. 4-10. Poly tape is an inexpensive way to weatherstrip windows, but the windows cannot be opened.

Fig. 4-11. To seal leaks at bottom of door, install a door sweep. This one has metal strip with three vinyl seals attached.

strip. It's also mounted on the door stops and the foam is compressed when the door closes to form a good tight seal.

If you find drafts or air leakage under the door, you may have to replace a worn wood threshold and add a metal strip with wood felt or flexible vinyl blade as a door sweep (Fig. 4-11) on the back of the door where it will be in contact with the floor or threshold. You may find it advantageous to substitute an aluminum threshold which interlocks with metal stripping on the door bottom. Other types have soft vinyl tubing against which the door closes, or a flexible vinyl "hump" which presses up against the bottom of the door when it is shut.

Weatherstripping At A Glance

Type of Material	What It Is/Where It's Used	Advantages & Disadvantages
Caulking cord	Soft, puttylike material in cord form that is pressed in place to seal wood/metal windows.	Inexpensive and easily installed, but only temporary. Once it is on, window may not be opened.
Poly tape	Clear self-adhering tape that seals wood/metal windows and patches cracked glass.	Inexpensive and easy; just press half on frame work, half on window. While it is on, window may not be opened.

continued on page 76

75

continued from page 75

Type of Material	What It is/Where It's Used	Advantages & Disadvantages
Duct tape	Strong adhesive-backed tape that may be used like poly tape on wood/metal windows.	Same as above, except that it comes in various sizes; it is also less attractive.
Felt	Strips of felt that are tacked or stapled on to plug the gap where windows or door meet the framework.	Inexpensive; easy to install if stapled on. Temporary; tends to deteriorate in time; may not be used successfully where parts slide against it.
Spring bronze	Spring-actuated strips of bronze that are nailed around wood door frame, creating a tight seal when door is closed.	Permanent weather stripping; but is difficult to install. Door must be planed down to accommodate it.
Steel interlocking	For use on wood doors. One part (on door) interlocks with other part (on framework).	Permanent; its protective metal framework foils burglars. Very difficult to install.
Serrated metal/felt combination	Felt encased in metal strips nailed around door or window framework to seal gaps.	Durable; works well on doors and windows that are opened often. not very attractive, and must be fastened with many small nails. (Tip: use brad driver.)
Plastic foam	Thick strips of foam to stuff into gaps between window sash or around air conditioner.	Easily installed—no fastening necessary; good for sealing extra large gaps, such as where window sash doesn't close completely. Temporary.
Self-adhering plastic foam	Adhesive-backed foam strips that adhere to framework where door or window meets it; work equally well on metal or wood.	Easily applied; sticks equally well to wood or metal. Not durable; wears where parts slide against it. Expensive.
Tubular vinyl gasket	Vinyl stripping with lip that nails to door or window frame to seal, or replaces weather strip in factory weather-stripped windows.	Durable and inexpensive. Slips easily into place on factory windows; hard to install (many nails needed) on standard windows.
Vinyl channel	Strips of U-shaped vinyl that slip over edge of metal casement windows.	Inexpensive, permanent, easily installed; window is free to open and close. Works only if window fits neatly and is not bent or otherwise distorted.
Wood and vinyl strips	Cut to size to form a standard door strip; vinyl on edge seals gap between door and frame.	Permanent, easily installed, attractive—can be painted. Door-closing noise is deadened.

continued on page 77

continued from page 76

Type of Material	What It Is/Where It's Used	Advantages & Disadvantages
Aluminum and vinyl strips	Aluminum strips with front edge of vinyl; install directly to face of standard door stop.	Same as above except that it is installed over existing door stop. Extremely durable.
Aluminum and vinyl door bottom	Aluminum part screws to bottom of wood door; vinyl part seals door/floor gap.	Extremely durable.
Rubber garage-door bottom	Molded double-lip strip nailed to bottom of garage door to seal door/floor gap.	Permanent weather stripping; cuts out drafts inside garage and cushions shock of door-
Aluminum saddle with vinyl gasket	Once saddle is installed on floor, vinyl gasket seals space between floor and closed door.	Effective when installed properly. Caution: Door bottom must be planed precisely to mate with saddle.
Aluminum saddle with interlocking door bottom	Saddle installed on floor and interlock installed on door bottom seal space when door is closed.	Easier to install than above; available in various sizes. It fits under any door. Interlock part can be troublesome, catching on rugs and carpeting as door moves.

Chapter 5
Why Ventilation is Important

Why Ventilation is Important

The less your cooling equipment has to work, the more money you are going to save. A most important aid is proper ventilation. Proper ventilation can, in many areas of the country, eliminate the need the homeowner has for air conditioning. It can also help eliminate excess winter moisture if this a problem.

MOISTURE IN THE HOME

The most important single area in your home to ventilate is the attic. Summer sun can easily push the temperature of the moist stagnant air in your attic as much as 60°F above the outside air, even if you have proper insulation.

This super-heated mass acts as a blanket over the entire house, working against your home or room air conditioners. Result: a heavier load on your cooling equipment, increased maintenance costs, high operating expenses and serious waste of energy. The solution is to replace trapped attic air with fresh, cool air from the outside with an efficient ventilating system.

The same solution applies to winter moisture. When it's cold outside, proper ventilation reduces the condensation that ruins insulation and boosts heating costs. Excess winter moisture stems from a number of sources, including various household appliances, such as dishwashers, dryers and humidifiers. Daily use of shower and tub, and cooking vapors also contribute to excessive moisture within the

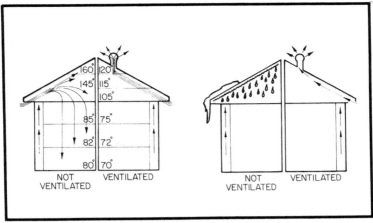

Fig. 5-1. Proper ventilation, left, removes hot air in summer, makes home cooler. Ventilator, right, carries moisture-laden air out of attic, prevents water damage.

home. Moisture-laden air rising from the living area to the attic condenses and causes problems (Fig. 5-1).

Besides soaking insulation and making it less efficient, excess moisture can stain or crumble ceilings, and blister exterior paint, Frozen and thawed, it can damage roof shingles.

There are a number of ways you can ventilate an attic, but it's best to have a basic understanding of how attic ventilation systems work first. In principle, there are two types of ventilation systems: 1) natural, or static, and 2) power systems. Some combinations of natural and power ventilation work better together than others.

TOTAL SYSTEM

Natural ventilation systems use fixed or nonmechanical devices referred to as ventilators. Installed in openings in the attic space, they must be properly positioned to take advantage of the natural flow of air.

Five basic types of attic ventilators exist: ridge, roof, under-eaves, gable end rectangular and triangular (Fig. 5-2). Ridge ventilators with undereaves strip ventilators are considered by experts to be the best natural ventilation system. Ridge vents provide a continuous opening along the entire ridge line of a pitched roof, keeping rain and snow out while allowing a full flow of air to be ventilated from the attic. Undereaves strip vents on both sides of the house are usually recommended when using ridge vents.

Roof vents with undereaves vents, say engineers, provide a good ventilation system for a hip style roof, while gable-end roofs may be equipped with either rectangular or triangular gable-end vents mounted in the high point of the gable. In all cases, undereaves intake ventilators complete the system.

A combination of power ventilators with undereaves vents for air intake provide an extremely effective attic venting system, according to engineers. They recommend this system for existing homes because it's easy to install. Some companies, for example, recommend either a continuous or 16″ × 18″ undereaves strip intake with power ventilators mounted on either a hip or gable roof.

POWER VENTILATORS

You can buy power ventilators (Fig. 5-3) which either install on the roof or on the gable sidewall. Roof types are typically placed on the rear slope of the roof, near the peak and centered, with air intakes at the eaves. This installation reaches all attic space efficiently. If locating it on the roof is either not practical or desirable, a power gable ventilator is the answer. Kits are available which are especially designed for easy installation by the do-it-yourselfer.

Attic power ventilators, available at building supply and home improvement centers, generally range from $50 to $150. They are available with thermostats which can be adjusted to start the power unit at a preset temperature of from 70°F to 160°F. The thermostat also shunts off the fan automatically when the attic temperature drops 15°.

Operating cost is minimal. A typical power ventilator, drawing about the same amperage as a 75-watt light bulb, can drop air conditioning costs from 10 to 30%. Engineers say exactly how much you'll save depends on your individual home and how you live. They point out that besides cutting operating costs, power vents may even allow you to get by with a smaller, lower-cost air conditioning system, or none at all.

Depending on what doors and windows are closed off, this can be a quite effective way of cooling a house, even on very hot summer days (Fig. 5-4). For example, in early morning, when outside air is still cool, the fan could be turned on until air in the house is cool, then shut down. Though outside air would heat, the interior of the house would still stay comfortably cool all day. Then, during the cool of night the fan could be turned on again.

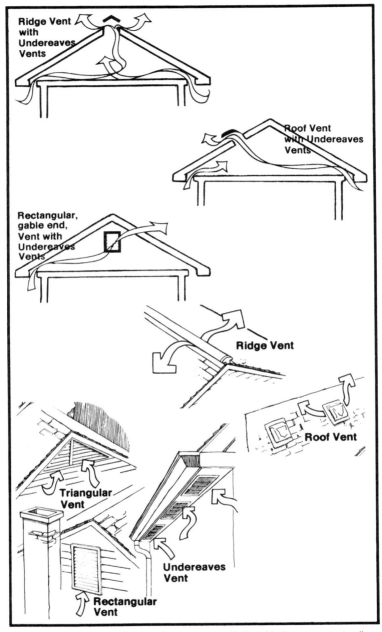

Fig. 5-2. Various types of vents allow cross-ventilation. Undereaves vents allow outside air in, while higher vents at roof, ridge or gable allow exhaust of attic air. Source: a Leigh brochure.

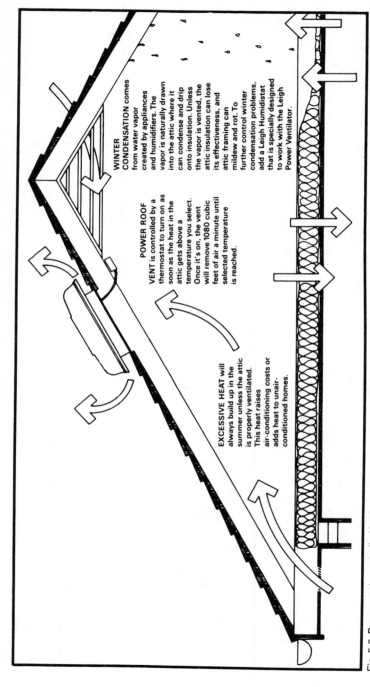

WINTER CONDENSATION comes from water vapor created by appliances and humidifiers. The vapor is naturally drawn into the attic where it can condense and drip onto insulation. Unless the vapor is vented, the attic insulation can lose its effectiveness, and attic framing can mildew and rot. To further control winter condensation problems, add a Leigh Humidistat that is specially designed to work with the Leigh Power Ventilator.

POWER ROOF VENT is controlled by a thermostat to turn on as soon as the heat in the attic gets above a temperature you select. Once it's on, the vent will remove 1080 cubic feet of air a minute until selected temperature is reached.

EXCESSIVE HEAT will always build up in the summer unless the attic is properly ventilated. This heat raises air-conditioning costs or adds heat to unair-conditioned homes.

Fig. 5-3. Power vents controlled by thermostat prevent excessive heat build-up in summer. In winter, humidistat on power units automatically corrects the vapor content of the attic so water doesn't drip on insulation or cause damage to attic framing. Source: a Leigh brochure.

84

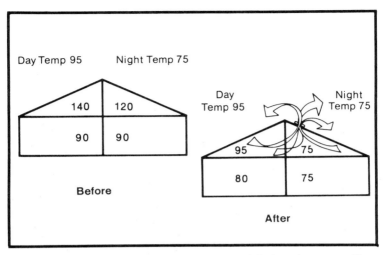

Fig. 5-4. Before, hot, stagnant and moisture-laden air in the attic warms ceilings below, making living and sleeping areas uncomfortable. After, power vent moves hot air out and fresh, cool air in. Unit safeguards shingles, paint and insulation. Source: Leigh.

It should be noted that the coolest air obtainable can usually be drawn from the bottom of the house. So, for example, you might want to use the whole house fan to pull cool air directly from the basement. Just leave the basement door, and other doors, open so you provide a direct route for the air to travel to the attic.

Window mounted fans can also be used for ventilation. Here, one should always try to set the fan so there is cross ventilation.

Before buying a power ventilator, figure how much ventilation is needed for your home by finding 1) the amount of free area needed for the system, and 2) the proper size of ventilator. The charts (Fig. 5-5) can help you figure both.

To figure free area needed (approximate clear or free opening of the ventilator through which air may move), first find the square footage of your attic floor. The space ventilated, say experts, should have a net free ventilated area ratio of 1/150. This means that for each 150 sq. ft. of attic floor space, 1 sq. ft. of free area is needed. In some cases, however, this ratio can be reduced to 1/300 (see top chart directions).

The bottom chart can help you find the proper size of power ventilator for your home. The Home Ventilating Institute (HVI), a recognized control agency, certifies air delivery of power attic space ventilators in cubic feet per minute (CFM). HVI standards recommend 10 air changes per hour, or a minimum of 0.7 CFM per sq. ft. of attic floor space, plus 15% for dark roofs.

Width (in feet)

Length (in feet)	20	22	24	26	28	30	32	34	36	38	40	42	44	46	48	50
20	192	211	230	250	269	288	307	326	346	365	384	403	422	441	461	480
22	211	232	253	275	296	317	338	359	380	401	422	444	465	485	506	528
24	230	253	276	300	323	346	369	392	415	438	461	484	507	530	553	576
26	250	275	300	324	349	374	399	424	449	474	499	524	549	574	599	624
28	269	296	323	349	376	403	430	457	484	511	538	564	591	618	645	662
30	288	317	346	374	403	432	461	490	518	547	576	605	634	662	691	720
32	307	338	369	399	430	461	492	522	553	584	614	645	675	706	737	768
34	326	359	392	424	457	490	522	555	588	620	653	685	717	750	782	815
36	346	380	415	449	484	518	553	588	622	657	691	726	760	795	829	864
38	365	401	438	474	511	548	584	620	657	693	730	766	803	839	876	912
40	384	422	461	499	538	576	614	653	691	730	768	806	845	883	922	960
42	403	444	484	524	564	605	645	685	726	766	806	847	887	927	968	1008
44	422	465	507	549	591	634	676	718	760	803	845	887	929	971	1013	1056
46	442	486	530	574	618	662	707	751	795	839	883	927	972	1016	1060	1104
48	461	507	553	599	645	691	737	783	829	876	922	968	1014	1060	1106	1152
50	480	528	576	624	672	720	768	816	864	912	960	1008	1056	1104	1152	1200
52	499	549	599	649	699	749	799	848	898	948	998	1048	1098	1148	1198	1248
54	518	570	622	674	726	778	830	881	933	985	1037	1089	1141	1192	1244	1296
56	538	591	645	699	753	807	860	914	967	1021	1075	1130	1184	1237	1291	1345
58	557	612	668	724	780	835	891	946	1002	1058	1113	1170	1226	1282	1337	1392
60	576	634	691	749	807	864	922	979	1037	1094	1152	1210	1267	1324	1382	1440
62	595	655	714	774	834	893	953	1012	1071	1131	1190	1250	1309	1369	1428	1488
64	614	676	737	799	861	922	983	1045	1106	1168	1229	1291	1352	1413	1475	1536
66	634	697	760	824	888	950	1014	1077	1140	1204	1268	1331	1394	1458	1522	1585
68	653	718	783	849	914	979	1045	1110	1175	1240	1306	1371	1436	1501	1567	1632
70	672	739	806	874	941	1008	1075	1142	1210	1276	1344	1411	1478	1545	1613	1680

FHA Chart   Chart utilizes 1/300 ratio; double for 1/150 ratio; divide by five for 1/1500 ratio.

WIDTH IN FEET

LENGTH IN FEET	20	22	24	26	28	30	32	34	36	38	40	42	44	46	48	50
20	280	308	336	364	392	420	448	476	504	532	560	588	616	644	672	700
22	308	339	370	400	431	462	493	524	554	585	616	647	678	708	739	770
24	336	370	403	437	470	504	538	571	605	638	672	706	739	773	806	840
26	364	400	437	473	510	546	582	619	655	692	728	764	801	837	874	910
28	392	431	470	510	549	588	627	666	706	745	784	823	862	902	941	980
30	420	462	504	546	588	630	672	714	756	798	840	882	924	966	1008	1050
32	448	493	538	582	627	672	717	761	806	851	896	941	986	1030	1075	1120
34	476	524	571	619	666	714	762	809	857	904	952	1000	1047	1095	1142	1190
36	504	554	604	655	706	756	806	857	907	958	1008	1058	1109	1159	1210	1260
38	532	585	638	692	745	798	851	904	958	1011	1064	1117	1170	1224	1277	1330
40	560	616	672	728	784	840	896	952	1008	1064	1120	1176	1232	1288	1344	1400
42	588	647	706	764	823	882	941	1000	1058	1117	1176	1234	1294	1352	1411	1470
44	616	678	739	801	862	924	986	1047	1109	1170	1232	1294	1355	1417	1478	1540
46	644	708	773	837	902	966	1030	1095	1159	1224	1288	1352	1417	1481	1546	1610
48	672	739	806	874	941	1008	1075	1142	1210	1277	1344	1411	1478	1546	1613	1680
50	700	770	840	910	980	1050	1120	1190	1260	1330	1400	1470	1540	1610	1680	1750
52	728	801	874	946	1019	1092	1165	1238	1310	1383	1456	1529	1602	1674	1747	1820
54	756	832	907	983	1058	1134	1210	1285	1361	1436	1512	1588	1663	1739	1814	1890
56	784	862	941	1019	1098	1176	1254	1333	1411	1490	1568	1646	1725	1803	1882	1960
58	812	893	974	1056	1137	1218	1299	1380	1462	1543	1624	1705	1786	1868	1949	2030
60	840	924	1008	1092	1176	1260	1344	1428	1512	1596	1680	1764	1848	1932	2016	2100
62	868	955	1042	1128	1215	1302	1389	1476	1562	1649	1736	1823	1910	1996	2083	2170
64	896	986	1075	1165	1254	1344	1434	1523	1613	1702	1792	1882	1971	2061	2150	2240
66	924	1016	1108	1201	1294	1386	1478	1571	1663	1756	1848	1940	2033	2125	2218	2310
68	952	1047	1142	1238	1333	1428	1523	1618	1714	1809	1904	1999	2094	2190	2285	2380
70	980	1078	1176	1274	1372	1470	1568	1666	1764	1862	1960	2058	2156	2254	2352	2450

HVI Chart   Chart utilizes 1/300 ratio; double for 1/150 ratio; divide by five for 1/1500 ratio.

Fig. 5-5. Charts are for figuring how much ventilation your home needs. Source: a Leigh brochure.

INSTALLATION STEPS

Power vents are easy to install yourself (Fig. 5-6). Gable units install easily behind gable-end vents. For roof vents, cut an opening, caulk the flange before nailing down the vent, and wire to standard house current. Equipped with thermostat, vent fan will start automatically when attic temperature reaches pre-selected setting. With optional humidistat, unit turns on automatically to rid attic of excess moisture. Here's a typical installation procedure:

1. For single unit installation, install unit close to center of length of roof. On flat roof installation, mount unit as close to the center of ventilated area as possible. Install multiple unit installations equally spaced over length of roof.

2. Establish ventilator location. Then drill or nail location hole through roof from inside of house. Center between rafters.

3. Locate nailed or drilled hole on roof. Cut away shingles and cut hole in roof. Apply roofing sealer in area between shingles and hole.

4. Remove interfering shingle nails. Remove ventilator hood, and slide vent up and under shingles. Center over 15″ circular cut-out. Apply sealant in all areas of possible leakage.

5. Drill proper holes for lag screws or machine bolts and secure wire motor braces. Seal all areas of possible leakage. Replace ventilator hood.

6. From inside of attic, fasten electrical junction box securely to rafter toward peak of roof.

7. With electricity shut off, make all wiring connections as shown to conform to code. Warning: If unit is for use on standard 110-120V, 60 Hz circuits, do not connect to any other voltage. This could result in personal injury. Also, do not oil permanently lubricated motors.

8. For best results, provide a minimum of 500 sq. in. of undereaves venting for each unit. Set unit thermostat at 100°F in northern half of U.S.; 110°F. in southern half.

WHERE ELSE

After you've installed an efficient power vent system in your attic, check for other areas of your house which may also require ventilation. Example: Basementless crawl spaces, as many owners

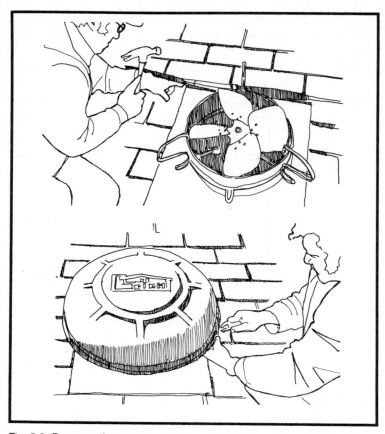

Fig. 5-6. Power roof vents are easy to install. Cut opening, caulk the flange before nailing down vent, and wire to standard house current. Complete instructions come with the unit. Source: Leigh.

know, attract humidity. Foundation ventilators or masonry ventilators let moisture escape from these areas instead of condensing on the flooring above. Engineers say such crawl spaces should have a net free ventilated area amounting to 1/150 of the ground area, except when the ground surface is covered with a vapor barrier. If covered, the ratio can be reduced to 1/1500 (see charts).

Walls also may need attention. Wall condensation problems can occur when moisture vapor inside the house seeps into hollow spaces in the walls. The moisture can work its way through to the outside walls and push exterior paint away from the siding, causing blisters and peeling.

Fig. 5-7. Place roofjack in position on roof near roof ridge, between rafters. Pencil circle inside to mark cutout.

Answer? Install paint breather vents or miniature circular louvered vents, both available at your building supply dealer. These vents are installed easily between stud spaces by simply drilling a hole of the same diameter as the vent and tapping the vents into place. Installing vents near the lower and upper parts of the outside wall provides an intake and outlet venting system.

Also check the laundry area in your home, a major source of humidity. Best solution here is to vent the dryer to the outside. *Caution:* Don't install a power vent to exhaust air from any space that is providing combustion air for fuel burning heating equipment. Improper combustion or inadequate venting could result and carbon monoxide could be produced.

PLANNING YOUR SYSTEM

You'll need some help in planning your system, so carefully read the instructions in the following sections.

Free Area Needed

The chart in Fig. 5-5 uses a 1/300 ratio (double for 1/150). Experts say you can use the 1/300 ratio if: 1) a vapor barrier is installed on the warm side of the ceiling, or 2) at least 50% of required ventilation area is provided by ventilators in the upper portion of the space to be ventilated (at least 3' above the under-eaves vents), with the remainder provided by undereaves vents.

To find exact free area needed to properly ventilate your home, find length of area to be ventilated in the vertical column and the width of the area in the horizontal column. Total net free area required is shown in sq. in. where the two columns intersect.

Sizing Power Vent

To find the size of ventilator needed to cool your attic efficiently, find length of area to be ventilated in the vertical column of the bottom chart, and the width of the area in the horizontal column. The total CFM required is shown where these two columns intersect. Double check your figures with the supplier when you buy your power unit.

Turbine Vents

The turbine-type vent requires no wiring; the exhaust is powered by winds turning the top, or turbine part, of the vent. The

Fig. 5-8. Cut shingles away with knife to avoid gumming sawblade. Hole may be cut with saber or keyhole saw.

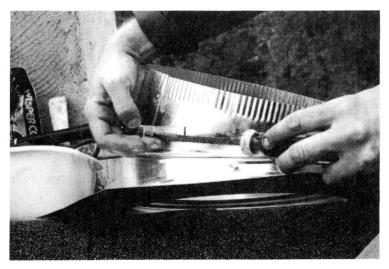

Fig. 5-9. Loosen screw, rotate upper and lower parts to adjust jack. This allows ventilator to set plumb on any roof pitch.

revolving turbine causes an updraft which pulls heat and moisture-laden air out of the attic.

To install the turbine vent (Figs. 5-7 through 5-12), locate it on the roof so that chimneys, trees or other obstacles do not interfere

Fig. 5-10. Place roofjack in place, level across top edges. Ventilator must be level to work properly.

Fig. 5-11. Apply a bead of roof mastic to edges on bottom side of flashing. Slip top edge of flashing under shingles above, nail jack in place with galvanized roofing nails.

with the free flow of air to the vent. Locate it near the top of the roof ridge; the top 8″ of the turbine should extend above the ridge.

Position the ventilator between roof rafters. Set the roof jack that will hold the turbine on the roof, and mark the hole's diameter

Fig. 5-12. Drill holes where roofjack and vent overlap. Secure with pop rivets or sheetmetal screws. Apply mastic at edges where shingles, flashing meet.

with a pencil. Cut out the circle for the vent using a keyhole or saber saw. Apply roof mastic on the flashing at the bottom of the roof jack. Then slip the roof jack in place, with the top edge of the flashing under the edges of the shingles above the hole. Nail the jack in place, using galvanized roofing nails.

A screw on the side of the roof jack allows the top of the jack to be rotated to offset the pitch of the roof. Turn the upper portion until the top of the jack is level from edge to edge. Tighten the adjustment screw so the jack will stay in this position. Set the turbine over the jack. Now drill four ⅛″ holes, equidistant around the perimeter of the ventilator, at the point where jack and turbine join. Secure the two together using sheetmetal screws or pop-rivets. Using roofing mastic, caulk around the juncture where shingles and ventilator jack meet.

Manufacturers recommend one turbine ventilator for each 600 sq. ft. of attic space. Since the idea is to pull outside air into the attic, and hot or moist attic air to the outside, it is important to provide 6 sq. ft. of louvers at soffits or eaves for each turbine ventilator.

Whole House Ventilating

Another type of powered ventilating system can be used to ventilate an entire house. Typically, an exhaust fan is installed in the ceiling of the top floor. It pulls outside air in through the windows and doors and exhausts it through the attic louver (this must be large) and provides breezes in the rooms with windows and doors. Finally, it prevents warm attic air from coming through ceilings into the living area.

Chapter 6
How You Can Trim Air Conditioning Costs

How You Can Trim Air Conditioning Costs

As with heating, there are a number of ways you can cut the costs of operating air conditioning and still keep cool. One of the first is to pick a size that's right for your needs. Invest some time in selecting a unit or units. If the cooling capacity of a room air conditioner is too small, it will not do an adequate job of cooling and dehumidifying. If it is too large, it may be more expensive to purchase and it may not dehumidify properly.

The cooling capacity of air conditioners is rated in Btu (British thermal units) per hour. This rating indicates the amount of heat an air conditioner will remove from the air each hour under specified test conditions. One Btu represents about the amount of heat produced by the burning of a wooden kitchen match to ashes. A room air conditioner with a cooling capacity of 5,000 Btu hour will remove approximately 5,000 Btu of heat from a room each hour.

CAPACITY RULE OF THUMB

The dealer can help you estimate what room air conditioner cooling capacity is needed for a given room. However, as a rule of thumb you can use a method (Fig. 6-1) developed by the Association of Home Appliance Manufacturers (AHAM):

1. First determine the square footage of the floor area to be cooled by multiplying the length by width.

2. Along the left side of the "Cooling Load Chart" shown, find the point corresponding to the room area.

Then move horizontally to the right of the center of Band A, B or C, depending on what kind of space is above the room to be cooled.

Band A—occupied room above is to be cooled;

Band B—insulated ceiling and unoccupied attic indicates an above room to be cooled;

Band C—uninsulated ceiling and unoccupied attic indicates an above room to be cooled.

3. From the center of the band, move horizontally within the band—to the left for a northern or shady exposure and to the right for a sunny exposure.

4. From this point move straight down to the bottom of the chart to determine the unadjusted cooling capacity in Btu per hour.

5. Locate your geographical area on the map and determine the climate factor for your area. Multiply the answer to No. 4 by the climate factor.

6. If the room is to be cooled primarily at night and the daytime temperature is not very important, multiply the answer to No. 5 by 0.7.

7. Determine the number of linear feet of wall separating the room to be cooled from other cooled rooms. Multiply this number by 30 Btu per hour and subtract the result from the answer to No. 5 (or No. 6 for night use).

8. If only one person will usually occupy the cooled room, subtract 600 Btu per hour from the answer to No. 7. If more than two people will usually occupy the room, add 600 Btu per hour for each person over two.

9. Add 4,000 Btu per hour to your answer in No. 8 if the area to be cooled includes a kitchen. The answer indicates the recommended cooling capacity of an air conditioner suitable for that room.

EXAMPLE

Consider the situation of choosing a room air conditioner for a 12′ × 15′ combined kitchen-dining area. An occupied room is above the kitchen. Northern exposure,

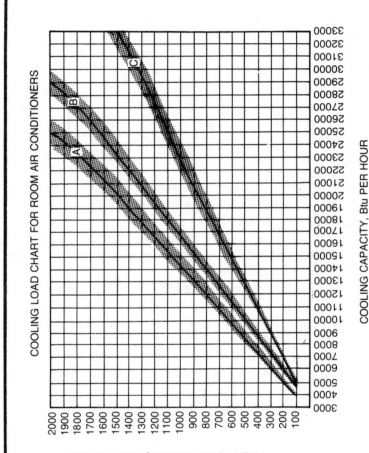

COOLING LOAD CHART FOR ROOM AIR CONDITIONERS

AREA TO BE COOLED, SQUARE FEET

COOLING CAPACITY, Btu PER HOUR

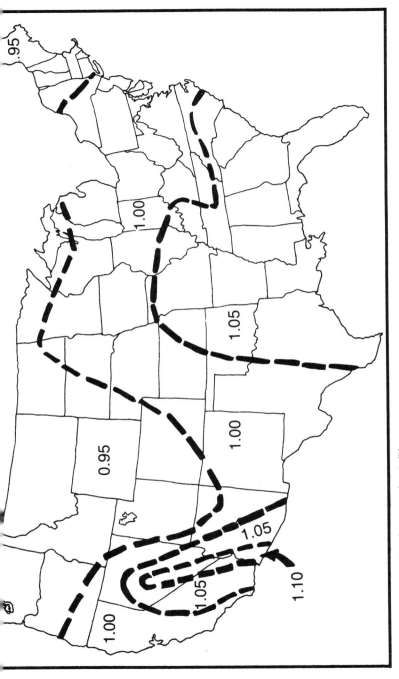

Fig. 6-1. Cooling load chart for room air conditioners.

with one 15' wall adjoining another cooled room. Normally occupied by one person during meal preparation. Located in Dallas, Texas.

1. The floor area 12' × 15' equals 180 square feet.
2. Find 180 on left side of chart and move horizontally over to center of Band A, since there is occupied space above the kitchen.
3. Move horizontally to left of Band A because the room has a northern exposure.
4. From the left edge of Band A, move straight down to bottom of chart. The unadjusted cooling capacity is 4,700 Btu per hour.
5. Since Dallas, Texas, has a climate factor of 1.05, multiply this by the answer to No. 4: (1.05 × 4,700 equals 4,935 Btu per hour).
6. Since the kitchen is to be cooled in the daytime, skip No. 6.
7. Since one kitchen wall adjoins another cooled room, multiply the length of that wall by 30 Btu per hour and subtract this from the answer to No. 5: (15 × 30 equals 450 Btu per hour; 4,935 minus 450 equals 4,485 Btu per hour).
8. Since there will normally be only one person in the kitchen during the peak heat load (food preparation), subtract 600 Btu from the answer to No. 7: (4,485 minus 600 equals 3,884 Btu per hour).
9. Since the room is a kitchen, add 4,000 Btu per hour to the answer to No. 8: (3,885 plus 4,000 equals 7,885 Btu per hour).

The required cooling capacity for the kitchen is about 8,000 Btu per hour. Models having cooling capacities between 7,500 and 8,500 Btu per hour would be suitable for this application.

COMPARING AIR CONDITIONERS

Once you have determined the cooling capacity you need, it is possible to judge how well different models of the same cooling capacity perform. This can be done by comparing the Energy Efficiency Ratio (EER) of various models. The EER is a measure of the amount of cooling a room air conditioner can do relative to the amount of electricity it uses.

Air conditioners with the same cooling capacity (as measured in Btu per hour) may vary greatly in efficiency. Some use much more electricity to achieve the same cooling and dehumidifying as others.

The EER is determined by dividing the Btu per hour rating of a room air conditioner by the watts it uses. Air conditioners with higher EER ratings are relatively more efficient; those with lower EER's are less efficient. For a given cooling capacity, the more efficient models consume less electricity and are less costly to operate. The EER rating will be on the machine.

OPERATING COSTS

The total cost to operate a room air conditioner for a season depends on the climate you live in, power requirement of your air conditioner, cost of electric service in your area, and such factors as the time of day and how frequently you leave the unit on and at what control settings.

Climate determines the number of hours each season you will have to operate your air conditioner to obtain the temperature reduction and dehumidification needed for comfort. The average yearly operation in some representative U.S. cities is shown below.

Estimated Annual Hours of Operation for Properly Sized Equipment During Normal Cooling Season

City	Hours/Season	City	Hours/Season
Atlanta, Ga.	750	Jacksonville, Fla.	1,600
Boston, Mass.	200	Minneapolis, Minn.	350
Chicago, Ill.	400	New Orleans, La.	1,500
Cleveland, Ohio	450	New York, N.Y.	350
Dallas, Texas	1,400	St. Louis, Mo.	1,000
Fresno, Calif.	900	Washington, D.C.	800

The machine's label will also state the power requirement of the unit in watts. This figure is obtained by measuring the unit's performance under standard test conditions. Electric service rates are based on the kilowatt-hour, which represents the usage of 1,000 watts of electrical power in one hour. The kilowatt-hours of electricity that a room air conditioner uses in a season can be calculated by multiplying the wattage rating of an appliance times the number of hours of usage per season (see chart) and dividing by 1,000.

Your electric service rate depends on local rates and the amount of electricity you use. For homeowners using between 500 and 1,000 kilowatt-hours of electricity per month, U.S. rates in a recent year varied from about 1¢ to 9¢ per kilowatt-hour; the national average was about 2.2¢ per kilowatt-hour. To find out your rate, call your local utility company.

You can estimate the cost of electricity to operate a room air conditioner in your home for one season by using the following formula:

Cost equals (your electric rate) × (hours operation per season) × (wattage rating/1,000)

For example, if you live in an area with a climate similar to that of Dallas, Texas, and if you are an average user, you may operate your room air conditioner about 1,400 hours per season (see chart). If your electric service rate is 3¢ ($.03) per kilowatt-hour, and the wattage rating of the room air conditioner you select is 860 watts, your estimated cost for electricity will be:

Cost equals .03 × 1,400 × $\dfrac{860}{1,000}$ equals $36.12 per season

This figure reflects average use. If you use your air conditioner only at night, you will operate it fewer hours and at lower outdoor temperatures, and your cost will be less. If you try to maintain an unusually low indoor temperature throughout the day, your cost will be greater. The higher you set the air conditioner's thermostat, the less time the unit will run and the lower your operating cost will be. Most people are comfortable at temperatures up to 80°F.

COMPARING EFFICIENCY

This method for estimating the cost of electricity to operate a room air conditioner can also be used to figure whether it is economically worthwhile to purchase a more efficient model with an initial cost that may be appreciably more than a less efficient model.

For example, assume that a relatively inefficient model is available on the market at a price of $60 lower than the model used in the example above. The ratings of the two models are as follows:

Efficiency Comparisons of Two Air Conditioners

Unit Characteristics	More Efficient Model	Less Efficient Model
Cooling capacity, Btu per hour	8,000	8,000
Power Requirement, watts	860	1,380
Energy Efficiency Ratio (EER)	9.3	5.8
Hours use—per season*.	1,400	1,400
Electricity cost per season*	$36.12	$57.96
*Estimated		

Based on these ratings, the estimated cost of electricity would be $21.84 per year lower for the more efficient model. If the more efficient model were priced $60 higher than the less efficient one, the higher price would be made up within three years by savings in the cost of electricity. In other areas, however, it may take much longer.

DO-IT-YOURSELF CENTRAL AIR

The above information on room air conditioners also applies to central air conditioning. It is usually true that central air conditioning will be less expensive than having units in individual rooms. You can greatly reduce costs of central air units by installing one yourself.

By buying a do-it-yourself package, and adding a day of your labor, you can have the comfort of central air at about 30% less than having it installed. Special central air packages for do-it-yourself homeowners have well-organized instructions. Back-up technicians usually are available in case you run into problems.

Installation is not diffiuclt. If you carefully follow directions, the only steps it will pay you to "hire out" include connection of the thermostat and hook-up from the fuse box to the outdoor condensing unit. A professional electrician can handle both jobs easily and quickly.

The Thomas A. Edison Do-It-Yourself Central Air Conditioning package shown here, from McGraw-Edison, contains:

1. *Condensing unit* with built-in disconnect switch that eliminates need for a special outdoor electrical box.
2. *Cooling coil* which fits into plenum of upflow furnaces.
3. *Pre-insulated refrigerant tubing kit* which includes lengths of sealed, pre-charged copper tubing, and quick-connect couplings.
4. *"One-trip" cooling coil installation kit* which includes sealing compound, plenum cover, adjustable coil support rods, and air baffles.

103

1

Complete this form.

One Story House

A. Multiply total area to be conditioned (length x width) to give you square feet.

_____ x _____

= _____ sq. ft.

(If your home has more than one story, subtract 30% of area which is located below air conditioned areas for your total square feet.)

2 Determine the temperature zone and zone multiplier from chart below:

State & City	Temp. Zone	Zone Mult.
ALABAMA	A	23
ARIZONA	B	26
except Flagstaff, Winslow	C	27
Yuma	C	27
ARKANSAS	A	26
except Texarkana	B	26
CALIFORNIA	A	23
except Bakersfield, Fresno. Red Bluff. Sacramento. San Bernardino	B	27
El Centro	C	27
COLORADO	A	23
CONNECTICUT	A	23
DELAWARE	A	23
DIST. OF COLUMBIA	A	23
FLORIDA	B	26
except Keywest	A	26
GEORGIA	A	21
except Augusta. Columbus	B	23
IDAHO	B	26
ILLINOIS	A	21
except Cairo	B	23
INDIANA	A	23
IOWA	A	23
except Council Bluffs	B	23
KANSAS	B	23
except Concordia. Dodge City	A	27
KENTUCKY	A	23
LOUISIANA	A	26
MAINE	A	23
MARYLAND	A	23
MASSACHUSETTS	A	23
MICHIGAN	A	23
MINNESOTA	A	23
MISSISSIPPI	A	26
MISSOURI		
Columbia. Kansas City. Springfield. St Joseph	B	26
Hannibal. Kirksville. St. Louis		
MONTANA	A	26
NEBRASKA	A	21
Grand Island. Hastings. North Platte. Omaha	B	23
Lincoln. Norfolk. Valentine. York		
NEVADA	B	26
except Las Vegas	A	21
NEW HAMPSHIRE	A	23
NEW JERSEY	A	23
NEW MEXICO	A	23
except Roswell	B	23
NEW YORK	A	23
NORTH CAROLINA	A	26
NORTH DAKOTA	A	23
OHIO	A	23
OKLAHOMA	B	27
except Muskogee	B	27
OREGON	A	21
PENNSYLVANIA	A	23
RHODE ISLAND	A	23
SOUTH CAROLINA	A	26
SOUTH DAKOTA	A	23
except Huron	B	23
TENNESSEE	A	26
TEXAS	A	27
except Austin, Dallas, Del Rio, El Paso, Fort Worth. Palestine. San Antonio. Waco	B	27
UTAH	A	23
VERMONT	A	23
VIRGINIA	C	27
WASHINGTON	A	23
WEST VIRGINIA	A	21
WISCONSIN	A	23
WYOMING	B	23
	A	26

Multiply the total square foot area from Step 1 by the zone multiplier to determine the BTU required. _____ sq. ft. x _____ = _____ BTU*

(found in **1**) (zone mult.)

NOTE: (1) If the area in which you reside is within 25 miles of the state line, and the adjoining state has a different temperature zone and multiplier, use the largest multiplier. (2) This "Short Form Evaluation" is applicable only to the equipment manufactured by McGraw-Edison Company, Air Comfort Division.

*This estimate is based on the average home of standard construction having normal glass area (20% of wall area), three inches or more of ceiling insulation, insulated sidewalls, roof overhang of 18 inches or more, or other type of shading that deflects sunlight on south windows, and materially reduces the sun on east and west windows.

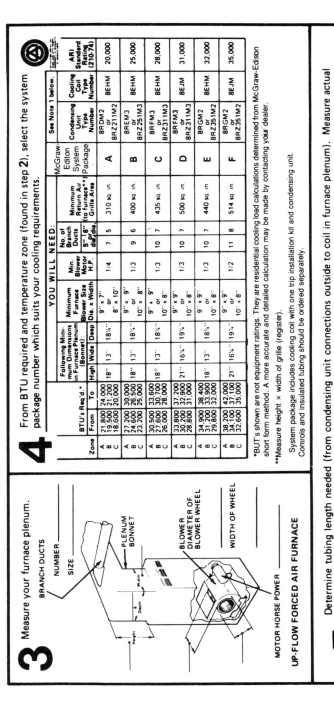

4

From BTU required and temperature zone (found in step **2**), select the system package number which suits your cooling requirements.

Zone	BTU's Req'd.* From	BTU's Req'd.* To	Following Minimum Dimensions in Furnace Plenum (Bonnet): High	Following Minimum Dimensions in Furnace Plenum (Bonnet): Wide	Following Minimum Dimensions in Furnace Plenum (Bonnet): Deep	Minimum Furnace Blower Size Dia. x Width	Min. Blower Motor H.P.	No. of Branch Ducts 5" dia.	No. of Branch Ducts 6" dia.	Minimum Return Air (to furnace**) Grille Area	McGraw-Edison System Package	Condensing Unit Type Number	Cooling Coil Type Number	ARI Standard Rating (210-74)
A	21,800	24,000	18"	13"	18¼"	9" x 7" or 8" x 10"	1/4	7	5	310 sq. in.	A	8RDM2 or 8RZ211M2	8EHM	20,000
B	19,500	21,200												
C	18,600	20,000												
A	27,200	30,000	18"	13"	18¼"	9" x 9" or 10" x 8"	1/3	9	6	400 sq. in.	B	8REM3 or 8RZ251M3	8EHM	25,000
B	24,600	26,500												
C	23,200	25,000												
A	30,500	33,600	18"	13"	18¼"	9" x 9" or 10" x 8"	1/3	10	7	435 sq. in.	C	8RFM3 or 8RZ311M3	8EHM	28,000
B	27,600	30,700												
C	26,000	28,000												
A	33,800	37,200	21"	16¼"	19¼"	9" x 9" or 10" x 8"	1/3	10	7	500 sq. in.	D	8RFM3 or 8RZ311M3	8EJM	31,000
B	30,800	32,900												
C	28,800	31,000												
A	34,900	38,400	18"	13"	18¼"	9" x 9" or 10" x 8"	1/3	10	7	440 sq. in.	E	8RGM2 or 8RZ351M2	8EHM	32,000
B	31,200	33,900												
C	29,800	32,000												
A	38,200	42,000	21"	16¼"	19¼"	9" x 9" or 10" x 8"	1/2	11	8	514 sq. in.	F	8RGM2 or 8RZ351M2	8EJM	35,000
B	34,400	37,100												
C	32,600	35,000												

| | YOU WILL NEED: | See Note 1 below. |

*BUT's shown are not equipment ratings. They are residential cooling load calculations determined from McGraw-Edison short form method. A more accurate and detailed calculation may be made by contacting your dealer.

**Measure height x width of grille (register).

System package includes cooling coil with one trip installation kit and condensing unit. Controls and insulated tubing should be ordered separately.

3

Measure your furnace plenum.

BRANCH DUCTS
- NUMBER _____
- SIZE _____

PLENUM BONNET

BLOWER DIAMETER OF BLOWER WHEEL

WIDTH OF WHEEL

MOTOR HORSE POWER _____

UP-FLOW FORCED AIR FURNACE

5

Determine tubing length needed (from condensing unit connections outside to coil in furnace plenum). Measure actual path tubing will take including bends around obstacles, etc. _____ (tubing length) ft.

(Insulated tubing comes in the following lengths: 15, 20, 25, 30, 35, 40 ft.)

Fig. 6-2. McGraw-Edison's five-step procedure will enable you to select the unit which will meet the cooling requirements for your furnace and home size.

5. *Accessory kit*, which includes heat/cool thermostat, leveling legs for condensing unit, and transformer-fan relay assembly.

6. *Installation manuals* which provide easy-to-follow instructions.

SELECTING CENTRAL AIR UNITS

Companies selling do-it-yourself units go to great lengths to make sure the unit you install meets cooling requirements for your furnace and home size. McGraw-Edison uses a five-step procedure (see Fig. 6-2) to make sure you get the right package.

First, you find the square footage of your home to be air conditioned. Total square feet is multiplied by a temperature zone factor. Next you measure your furnace plenum, blower diameter, width of wheel, and find furnace motor horsepower and the size and number of branch ducts. All these figures combine to give the size of the condenser and cooling unit you'll need for maximum cooling.

Don't fall into the trap of asking for a unit that's oversized for your house and furnace blower capacity. Bigger, in this case, is not necessarily better. Larger units don't cycle often enough to effectively dehumidify your house. Size the system so it operates long enough to do a good job of dehumidifying.

Final step before buying is to measure the distance from your furnace to the spot where the condensing unit will be located outside your house. This is to determine the exact length of pre-charged copper tubing needed to connect the condensing unit (Fig. 6-3) and the cooling coil. The condensing unit should be located as close as possible to the furnace, facing away from the house to the most distant corner of your lot. The distance between condensing unit and cooling coil should not exceed 40'.

TIPS ON INSTALLING

With these figures in hand you're ready to contact your dealer who will specify the correct kit for your home. From there on, you follow step-by-step installation (see Fig. 6-4) up to connecting the 220V electrical hookup. Hiring an electrician for this hook-up will help you make sure local codes are met.

Most kits available are designed for upflow furnaces. They aren't recommended for downflow systems, and can't be used with hot water or steam heat systems.

106

Little maintenance is required to operate the units once they're installed. And they don't have to be removed during the heating season. A thermostat with a heat and cool setting will operate your air conditioner and furnace, but not at the same time. Properly installed, the system will not require recharging or additional refrigerant. If the unit loses refrigerant through a leak in the system, a refrigeration technician can be called to repair the leak and to add new refrigerant.

You can expect an air conditioner to add at least the cost of the system in real value, and make your home more attractive to potential buyers.

OPERATING TIPS

You can help an air conditioner operate at top efficiency by knowing what to do. Try to limit, as much as possible, the penetra-

Fig. 6-3. Installing central air conditioning can save up to $300 in outside labor charges if you do it yourself. The only two-man requirement is setting up the condensing unit outside the house. Weighing just over 200 lbs., the unit should be blocked and leveled before you begin installing the cooling coil in the plenum chamber.

1 Initial hole is made above the furnace plenum by driving a screwdriver through the metal and then sideways to create an opening large enough for the tin snips.

2 Using a tin snips or saber saw, cut a large inspection hole in the plenum.

3 Insert a trouble light inside the chamber and measure the height of the duct flanges on the inside of the plenum.

4 Score two sets of lines on the outside of the plenum chamber using a level for accuracy. One set of lines should be the size of the coil cover; the second ½'' smaller.

5 Place the coil cover on the lines, then mark and drill holes that hold bolts to secure the cover.

6 Using the tin snips or saber saw, cut the square opening (inside lines) in the plenum. Install the adjustable coil rods over the duct flanges. These rods will support the coil.

7 Measure and cut cooling coil baffles to the proper size.

continued on page 109

continued from page 108

8 Install the baffles around the edges of the plenum where the cooling coil will rest. These baffles direct all air to be cooled through the coil.

9 Place sealing compound around the edges of the plenum and on edges of baffles where the cooling coil will rest.

10 Carefully position the cooling coil so tubing connections are opposite the holes left for them in the coil cover.

11 Screw the coil cover in place and connect the pre-charged tubing to the coil.

12 A drain line is required to drain condensate from the coil. It should be routed to the nearest floor drain.

13 Condensing unit, placed outside the house, is connected to the pre-charged tubing.

14 Complete operation, done in less than a day, can save you $200 to $300 in labor.

Fig. 6-4. Step-by-step instructions for installing central air conditioning.

tion of heat into the house. Your main line of defense is insulation, weatherstripping and storm windows. But there is a grab bag of other things that, collectively, will make a big difference, too:

- Use blinds and draperies to reduce heat gain through windows as much as 50%. The effectiveness of blinds and draperies depends on how well they reflect solar radiation. They should be light in color and opaque. Open-weave draperies are less effective but do allow good ventilation.
- Use special heat absorbing and reflecting glass. These also reduce solar heat through windows appreciably, but don't interfere with the view.
- Use awnings and overhangs. These represent the most effective way to reduce solar heat gain. They must be porperly designed, however, to prevent hot air from being trapped beneath them.
- Shade the house from the sun by planting fast-growing trees or large shrubs around the home. Deciduous trees (those that lose their leaves in winter) have the special advantage of providing summer shade and allowing maximum exposure to the sun in cold weather.
- If your house has central air conditioning, set thermostats at 79°F. Turning up the thermostat to this temperature, rather than to 73°F., can bring substantial savings. Exact energy savings depend on where you live, but for every 20°F. that the thermostat is turned up figure on an energy savings of 18% or more.
- If the circuilation fan on your room air conditioner has more than one speed, run it at lower speeds in mild weather. Since most houses have enough natural air leakage for ventilation, the outdoor air damper should be closed for greater effectiveness and economy; it can be opened to speed up removal of cooking or tobacco odors. Turn the unit off if rooms are unoccupied for several hours.
- Locate the thermostat control of a central air conditioning system on an inside wall where comfort is most important, or in a hallway where it can sense air circulating from several rooms.
- Reduce heat generation in the house. Overall, the average heat generation produced (excluding heat given off by oc-

cupants) in a moderately sized household might be 60,000 Btu per day or more. Limit the use of appliances and lighting as much as possible.

- Turn off lights when not needed, especially high wattage lights used for sewing, study, hobbies, etc. Use daylight (not direct sunlight) from windows whenever practical and use lighter colors on interior wall surfaces to reflect natural daylight.

- Use the most efficient and practical light sources. Fluorescent tubes give more light than incandescent lamps for a given amount of electricity and they generate less heat. (It is not a good idea, however, to run fluorescent lights off and on if you leave the lighted area for brief periods, such as 10 minutes or so. Repeated starting of fluorescent tubes shortens their lifespan).

- Turn off television sets, radios, and phonographs when no one is paying attention to them. Limit use of electric irons, hair dryers, and other electrical appliances.

- Make sure that refrigerator or freezer door seals are air tight and that their condensing coils are clean for good air flow. Avoid unnecessary or prolonged door openings.

- Don't activate the cleaning feature of self-cleaning ovens at times when air conditioning loads are heavy. Operate self-cleaning feature late at night or early in the day.

- Try to confine heavy use of showers, cooking, clothes drying, and ironing to the cooler morning or evening hours. When cooking, cook several dishes or whole meals in the oven at the same time to limit oven use. Use cooking pots of the same diameter as the stove burner or heating coil, and use covered pots and low fires whenever possible, especially when boiling. Keep oven doors closed when cooking and check seal of oven gasket seals to make sure that heat is not leaking out.

- Activate kitchen or bath exhaust fans (if vented to the outside when there is a large amount of water vapor or heat due to cooking, bathing, or washing), rather than opening windows when the air conditioning is on. Close off rooms in which exhaust fans are used to prevent air conditioned air from being exhausted to the outside. Remember to turn off the fans when the job is done.

CLOSE UP TO SAVE ENERGY

Close and seal all openings into the attic from occupied space, including cracks around attic doors, to prevent hot attic air from seeping into air conditioned areas or cooler areas of the house. Close off rooms and closets not in use to avoid needless cooling of unused space. Also keep windows and doors shut and keep storm windows and doors in place when the air conditioning system is turned on. If the house has a fireplace, don't forget to close its damper to prevent the entry of warm outside air. Remember, too, the value of attic venting of the house—this can reduce the need for air conditioning.

AIR CONDITIONER MAINTENANCE

Regular maintenance by the do-it-yourselfer and the serviceman will keep an air conditioner operating at peak efficiency. Make sure the condenser is clean. Check it for leaves and other debris. If possible, it's also a good idea to keep it shaded.

Inspect the air filter at least twice during the summer. Most air filters that are made of aluminum or rubber mesh can be washed in soapy water or vacuum cleaned. The fibrous type usually must be replaced. Check your owner's manual.

Further, make sure your serviceman periodically performs the following maintenance:

- Lubricate bearings and fan if they are not sealed.
- Measure current drawn by the compressor.
- Check pulley belt tension.
- Check for refrigerant leaks.
- Check electrical connections.
- Adjust dampers on central air conditioning. Here, different settings are usually required for cooling than for heating.
- Flush evaporator drain line.

Chapter 7

What You Should Know

About Heating Systems

What You Should Know About Heating Systems

One of the easiest of the economical ways to save money on home heating is to use the thermostat to avoid wasting energy. Consider doing the following:

1. Turn down the thermostat to 65–68°F when the home is occupied during the heating season.
2. Set back the thermostat to 60°F at night during the heating season.
3. Set the thermostat to a low position (45–55°F) when the home will not be occupied for extended periods, such as during winter vacations.
4. Turn off the pilot light during the nonheating season. (Note: when relighting, follow lighting instructions closely.)

Another excellent way to save energy is to keep your heating system in top operating condition. Like a well-tuned car, a good heating system tuneup can cut back fuel bills 10–15%. Typically a heating system consists of an oil or gas furnace (Fig. 7-1) for generating heat, and a system for distributing it, either forced warm air (the most common), hot water or stream. Electric heating is also popular, but generally this kind of system offers fewer opportunities to the do-it-yourselfer except for keeping the heating surfaces clean.

There are some things you can do to get your furnace in shape, but other aspects of maintenance should be left to a serviceman.

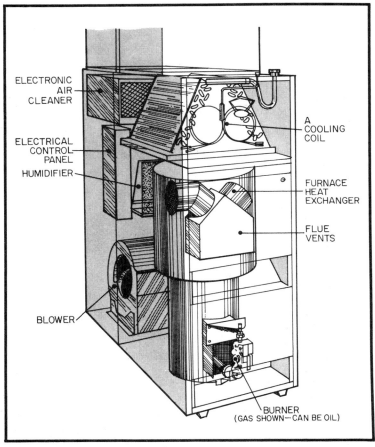

ELECTRONIC
AIR
CLEANER

ELECTRICAL
CONTROL
PANEL

HUMIDIFIER

BLOWER

A
COOLING
COIL

FURNACE
HEAT
EXCHANGER

FLUE
VENTS

BURNER
(GAS SHOWN—CAN BE OIL)

Fig. 7-1. Forced warm air furnaces consist of furnace, ducts and registers. Blower in furnace circulates warm air to various rooms through supply ducts and registers. Cooled room air is carried back to furnace through return grilles and ducts, then reheated and recirculated.

Most jobs you can perform fall into the area of cleaning and lubricating.

OIL BURNERS

First, motors should be properly lubricated. This includes the oil pump and the blower motor if your home has a forced-air distribution system (Fig. 7-2). Before doing any oiling, consult your owner's manual. Not all blower motors require lubricating. Most new blower units are made pre-lubricated and sealed.

115

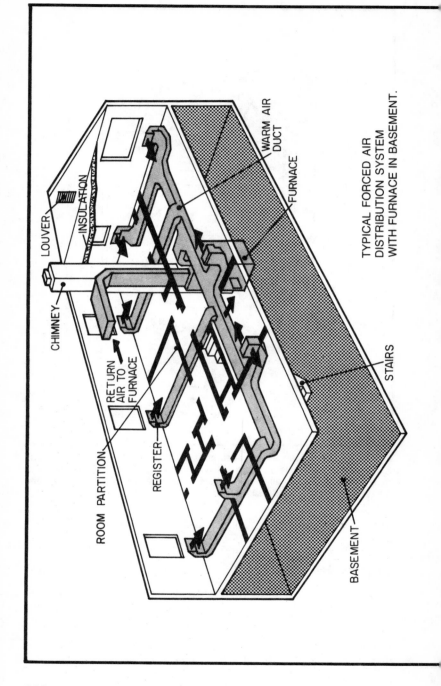

LOUVER

CHIMNEY

INSULATION

RETURN
AIR TO
FURNACE

ROOM PARTITION

REGISTER

WARM AIR
DUCT

FURNACE

STAIRS

BASEMENT

TYPICAL FORCED AIR
DISTRIBUTION SYSTEM
WITH FURNACE IN BASEMENT.

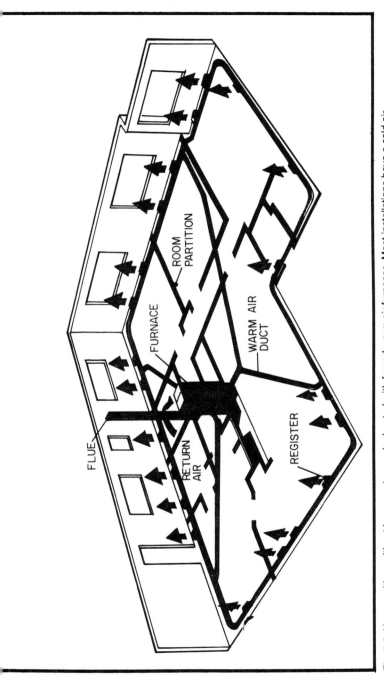

Fig. 7-2. Homes with or without basements may be heated with forced warm air furnaces. Most installations have a cold air return in each room except bathroom and kitchen as shown at top. Perimeterloop heating systems, bottom, are often used in basementless homes built on concrete slabs.

If yours is not of this type, check the manual for location of oiling points. There will usually be two of these, one at each end of the blower motor. On some units the second bearing may be hard to reach. However, most blowers are mounted on a slide-out device (secured with a screw or two) which allows you to reach the inside oiling point. Be sure to retighten blower screws.

For oiling any motors, buy an engineer's oil can with a spout and a "pump" lever on the handle. It will let you reach difficult areas easier. Use only a drop or two of oil at intervals suggested by your manufacturer, but at least every 60 days during the heating season. Use 30 weight machine oil; non-detergent motor oil will do.

There is an oil filter in the feeder system to clean oil before it goes to the burner. It should be on the back end of the pump unit. Periodically (and anytime your furnace sputters or operates inter-mittently) clean this filter by (1) shutting off the electric power switch, (2) removing about six bolts from the top of the unit, (3) lifting out filter, and (4) washing it gently in kerosene. In lieu of cleaning the filter, replace it with a new one. Clean off the blower vanes (Fig. 7-3).

OIL FURNACE CLEANUP

Furnace flues should also be periodically checked and cleaned, if necessary. (Generally gas furnaces will not need to be cleaned.) Check your owner's manual to determine the location of access openings to flue passages, then follow this procedure. (1) Turn thermostat to lowest position. (2) Close all valves on lines between the oil tank and furnace. (3) Shut off electricity to the furnace.

Typically the front door is removed from the furnace and the flue box cover is taken off. Behind that is a cover or covers which allow access to the flue (Fig. 7-4).

To clean the flue, insert a vacuum cleaner nozzle as far back into the flue as possible then simply turn the machine on. If you do this job annually, dirt will not build up to a point where the specialized equipment used by a serviceman is needed. After cleaning, replace covers, open valves and turn electricity back on.

On a warm air system it is important to keep ducts, registers and filters clean because the blower cannot operate efficiently through a dirty system. Remove the cover over the blower unit of your furnace, then the filter. Vacuum away dust in the return air

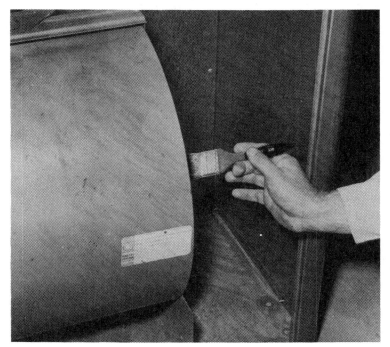

Fig. 7-3. Small brush is useful to clean vanes around blower on forced warm air system. A small dirt buildup on the fan blades will reduce the blower capacity.

blower compartment, and off the blower unit. Clean filters are easily installed and will minimize this problem. Buy extra filters to have on hand for replacement as necessary.

Also remove the registers and vacuum away dust on the back of them, as far into the duct as you can reach. If you do this twice a year (once while the furnace is shut down, and again at the mid-point of the heating season), you will seldom need professional cleaning.

Tip: Watch filters (Fig. 7-5) and registers (Fig. 7-6) for dirt build-up. If this is infrequent, you don't need the ducts cleaned by a pro.

Registers should be of the diffusion type to eliminate a direct draft. If you're getting dirt streaks around the register covers, replace the rubber gasket that fits between the register and wall. These can be made by using the narrow peel and stick weatherstripping material of sponge rubber. If you have a "cold spot" in your house that cannot be corrected by tuning your furnace (described

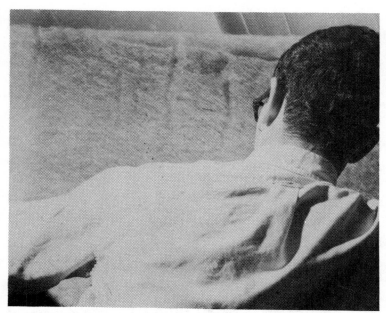

Fig. 7-4. Typical arrangement of oil-fired heat exchanger cleanout. Getting to it and cleaning flue is a job you can do.

Fig. 7-5. Hold filters up to light to check cleanliness. Filters should be replaced frequently so duct and blower assembly operates efficiently. Walls and furnishings will stay cleaner, too.

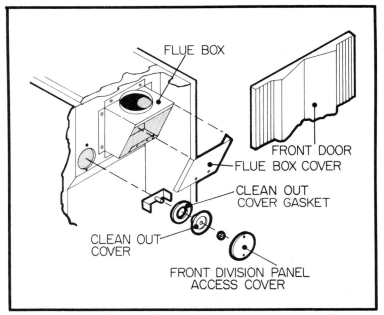

FLUE BOX

FRONT DOOR

FLUE BOX COVER

CLEAN OUT
COVER GASKET

CLEAN OUT
COVER

FRONT DIVISION PANEL
ACCESS COVER

Fig. 7-6. Use long brush and vacuum to clean ducts after removing registers.

below), you can buy booster fans that insert into the duct or are installed as a fan/register unit.

TUNING DUCTS

The furnace installer will tune the dampers in your ducts to an approximate balance, so heat flow will be adjusted for all areas of the house. However, dampers may need to be readjusted in both new and older homes to get the proper balance. This tuning consists of turning dampers wide open on the longest runs from furnace to register and partially closing dampers on runs where register to furnace distance is short.

Tip: If you are shutting off the heat in unused portions of the home, do it at the duct damper instead of the register. The furnace is still pushing heat down the duct if you close the register.

PROFESSIONAL SERVICING

To give you an idea of what the serviceman can do to get your furnace in shape, below is a listing of typical maintenance procedures and tests.

OIL BURNER SERVICING

- Replace the fuel nozzle and check the electrode setting on the burner (Fig. 7-7). (The nozzle and electrode assembly is reached by removing the assembly access cover.) Yearly nozzle replacement is a good idea because it guards against the possibility of its small aperture becoming clogged. A nozzle costs only about $1.50. Electrodes don't usually lose their adjustment, but replacing the nozzle can accidentally jar it out of proper setting. Unhappily even slight deviation can affect ignition. Electrodes are generally set ⅛″ to 3/16″ apart.

- Check the furnace oil-pumping pressure. Pumping pressure determines the amount of fuel delivered to the combustion chamber. If pumping is excessive, fuel atomization will be too fine. If there isn't enough pressure, fuel droplets will be too large. Acceptable pumping pressure for most oil burners is 100 to 105 lbs. per sq. in. (psi).

- Check stack temperatures in the vent beyond the heat exchanger. Normal stack temperature is 500–750°F on all furnaces and 300–500°F on gas furnace stacks. All previously tested heating equipment will already have a small hole drilled in the side of the stack. A stack thermometer (good up to 1000°F) is inserted to take a direct reading.

- Test for CO_2. The best fuel/air ratio will result in the highest CO_2 readings and the highest efficiency (Fig. 7-8). Excess

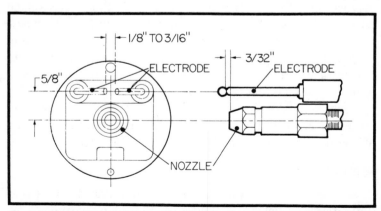

Fig. 7-7. Electrode assembly on oil burner. Replacing nozzle (a job for service-man) is inexpensive and should be done at start of each heating season.

Fig. 7-8. A CO_2 test determines best fuel/air ratio. This also is test that should be done by a serviceman.

air must be available in the combustion chamber to make sure all the fuel is burned and the heat released. Too much excess air cools the products of combustion and reduces efficiency. The test is done by taking a sample of flue gas to determine the CO_2 reading.

The combustion efficiency can be read from a chart when the stack temperature and CO_2 reading are known. The normal 75% efficiency indicates 75% of the fuel's heat goes into the building and 25% goes out the vent. Some of the stack heat is required to expel the products of combustion. That heat is used and not "wasted."

• Test smoke density. This is an adjunct to the CO_2 test and allows the serviceman to determine if excessive fuel is being burned. It is done by subjecting a piece of special filter paper to a sampling of flue gas. The filter paper is compared with a gauge to visibly determine if smoke is too dense. If so, the fuel mixture is leaned by increasing the air intake.

• Check for proper draft. This is done with a gauge called an incline manometer. The test is made at two places: at the front door over the fire and in the smoke pipe. Typically, good draft at the burner door is about 0.02″ while good draft in the exhaust stack is 0.06″. If there isn't enough draft, it indicates that the chimney or flue passages are plugged with soot. Too much draft suggests that a regulator or stack adjustment is needed. (Gas furnaces are atmospheric burners and these pressures do not apply. Draft can be checked with cigarette smoke at the draft hood relief opening.)

GAS FURNACE SERVICING

For the most part, the same jobs and tests made on an oil burner are made when tuning up a gas furnace and, of course, the heat distribution system should be handled the same way. Make sure you read the oil burner section concerning the stack temperatures, test for CO_2 and combustion efficiency.

Note: Do not attempt to adjust the controls or burner flame unless you have expertise in these areas. Have a furnace man or your gas company serviceman clean and adjust the burner, and regulate pressure. If pilot gas pressure is set too high, or "sharp," the pilot light will not stay lit. If it's too "soft," you'll get undue soot build-up in your exhaust stack.

To complete servicing, the service technician should check out the overall performance of the furnace in conjunction with the system's delivery system, either steam, hot water, or forced warm air.

If the system is steam or hot water, the technician should adjust controls, such as the boiler limit switch and steam pressure regulator. He should also test and lubricate the circulator of a hot water system.

STEAM SYSTEM SERVICING

If your home has steam, the boiler blow down should be periodically flushed. Turn on the valve on the water line to the boiler, then turn on the valve on the low water cut off, letting the water run out until clear (Fig. 7-9).

If you have radiators, check to see that all of them get hot without making noise. If heat is reduced or there is knocking, there is likely a buildup of air. Use a screwdriver or dime to turn the valve until the air hisses out and water flows (have a cup handy) (Fig. 7-10).

Also check the radiator water shut-off valve to see if water is dripping from the control. Dripping water indicates deteriorated packing. To renew it, turn the handle and pacing nut to maximum

Fig. 7-9. Steam boiler low water cutoff system should be blown down to remove sediment.

height, wrap packing material around the threads (one or two turns is sufficient) and then turn the hardware back in place (Fig. 7-11).

Regardless the system you have, check the unsealed contact points on the thermostat. Dust or dirt may build up here and cause the furnace to fail. You may clean the points by pulling a business card between them. Most thermostats made in the last 10 years have sealed contacts that don't require servicing.

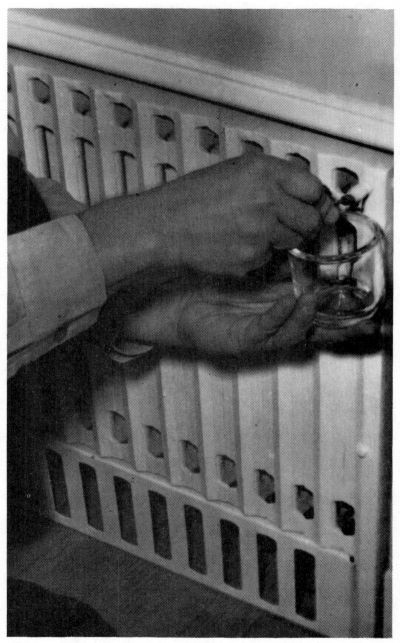

Fig. 7-10. If radiators on hot water system make noise or don't heat up properly, bleed system of air by turning valve until water flows.

Fig. 7-11. Leak around valve stem can often be fixed with ordinary faucet packing. Wrap a few turns around stem, tighten nut.

Perhaps the most important thing the homeowner can do, beyond keeping the furnace cleaned and oiled, is to visually inspect the furnace on at least a weekly basis during the heating season. Any strange noise, or the presence of soot or rust on burner, heat stack, vent connector or around the exhaust vent from a gas water heater indicates problems that should get attention.

Chapter 8
Humidity Control
Can Save You Money

Humidity Control Can Save You Money

As Chapter 5 explains, getting excess heat and moisture out of the house will go a long way towards economizing on cooling costs. In the winter, most people has the opposite problem: there's not enough moisture in the air. Indeed, the air is very dry. This makes you feel colder, which will make you turn up the heat, and will sap moisture from the respiratory tract, as well as furnishings and the house itself (Fig. 8-1).

The answer is a humidifier, which introduces measured amounts of moisture into the air. Let's take a closer look.

HUMIDITY IN THE HOME

Air becomes drier as it is heated. Suppose you heat air having a temperature of 10°F and a relative humidity of 70% to 72°F. At 72°F the ability of that air to hold moisture is increased by over 300%. In other words, when you heat 10°F, 70% relative-humidity air to 72°F, the relative humidity of the air drops to only 6%, which is extremely dry.

Yet the relative humidity of air in the average American home during the heating season is not much more than this. It averages out to be 13%, which is twice as dry as the air in the Sahara Desert (26%).

"When we breathe dry air with low relative humidity, localized areas of dryness and desiccation will occur on the surface of the respiratory membrane," Charles S. Sale, M.D., and director of the American Humidification Foundation, points out. "Without doubt," he states, "dryness of the respiratory membrane is the major cause of most colds and respiratory illness during the winter months."

Dry air adversely affects practically everything in the home. The structure and nearly everything in it are hygroscopic materials, which means they are capable of absorbing moisture vapor from the air around them, and conversely, of releasing moisture to the air, depending on the relative humidity indoors. Some materials shrink significantly as they lose water in the presence of dry air, which causes them to warp and crack. The following happens:

- Glue holding parts of tables, chairs and other furniture dries, causing them to loosen, joints to separate and cracks to appear.
- Plaster or gypsum wallboard dries out and cracks.
- Joists and studs shrink, leading to contorted and cracked walls.
- Pianos, organs and other musical instruments lose tone and crack.
- Floorboards shrink and separate and start to squeak.
- Books and pieces of art dry out and crack or break.
- House plants droop and become sick looking. Even desert plants, such as cactuses, do best at a relative humidity level of 40–50%.

According to experts, including the Air-Conditioning and Refrigeration Institute (ARI), the ideal humidity level inside a home heated to 70°F should be 30–40% (20–30% if it is below zero outside). If air in your home isn't at this level during winter, then you should consider the addition of a humidifier. Remember that humidification costs energy. Each pound of water vaporized requires over 1,000 Btu. The vaporization of one gallon of water requires about 10,000 Btu.

There are several ways of determining the level of humidity in a home. The "scientific" way is to buy a calibrated hygrometer or a sling psychrometer which measures the humidity level. An accurate instrument costs about $20.

Another way—one which won't cost you a penny—of telling whether the humidity level is too low is to conduct the ice cube test in your living room on a typically cold day when your heating system is operating. Put three ice cubes in a glass, add water, stir and wait

Fig. 8-1. Without humidification, dry air feels colder, which leads to higher thermostat settings. Dry air also can contibute to respiratory problems and damage to the physical structure of the home and furnishings.

three minutes. If moisture (or condensation) doesn't form over the glass, the indoor humidity level is too low.

Still another indication of the need for a humidifier is excessive static electricity in winter. People get a shock when touching an object or another person in your house.

If windows usually steam up during the coldest weather, the humidity level is too high for the house. It needs more window insulation. Colder climates will require storm windows before proper levels of humidity can be built up without steaming. Storm windows, weatherstripping and tight houses retain the moist air. The air flow through a loosely constructed house can sweep the humidity outside without any buildup inside. Most humidifiers wouldn't be able to maintain good humidity levels under those conditions.

CHOOSING A HUMIDIFIER

Humidifiers are available as small tabletop models (commonly called room vaporizers), portable floor models and central units that are attached to a forced hot air heating system. A central system humidifier works by evaporating moisture into the air flowing through the heating system. The furnace fan circulates the humidified air through the home. Some experts don't recommend the spray type humidifier. If the water is hard, white particles of calcium and magnesium will coat the inside of the ductwork—and maybe the house.

Fig. 8-2. This symbol appearing on a central system humidifier or in the accompanying literature attests that the unit is capable of doing what the manufacturer claims it will.

A central system humidifier can be used only with a forced hot air heating system. If your home is equipped with hot water, steam or electric heating and you decide you need humidification, one or more portable floor units must be used.

In 1973, the Air-Conditioning and Refrigeration Institute began a certification program to assure that the manufacturer's claim for capacity of a particular unit was accurate and that the unit met industry-wide performance and safety standards.

To be protected, you should look for the symbol of certification when buying a central system humidifer. The symbol of certification attests that the unit meets ARI Standard 610, and may appear on the model or in the manufacturer's literature and advertising (Fig. 8-2).

If you don't see the symbol, ask your dealer or contractor to show you the model listing in the *ARI Directory of Certified Central System Humidifiers*. Only certified equipment is listed.

The ARI program does not apply to portable room humidifiers. The certification program established by the Association of Home Appliance Manufacturers (AHAM) does apply, however, so look for the AHAM seal of assurance on these units.

When buying a central system humidifier, its capacity is an important consideration. Capacity—that is, output requirement— depends primarily on the size and tightness of your home.

The technical literature accompanying each model will inform you of the unit's capacity (certified by ARI). Discuss the capacity with the salesperson to determine if the unit will service the area.

Keep in mind that, from the standpoint of adding humidity to a home in winter, it is better to buy a unit that provides excessive capacity than one which has less capacity than is needed. A relative humidity level of 50% or even 60% in a home during the winter is suitable only for mild climates (Fig. 8-3).

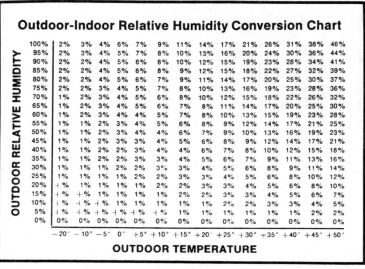

Outdoor-Indoor Relative Humidity Conversion Chart

OUTDOOR RELATIVE HUMIDITY	−20°	−10°	−5°	0°	+5°	+10°	+15°	+20°	+25°	+30°	+35°	+40°	+45°	+50°
100%	2%	3%	4%	6%	7%	9%	11%	14%	17%	21%	26%	31%	38%	46%
95%	2%	3%	4%	5%	7%	8%	10%	13%	16%	20%	24%	30%	36%	44%
90%	2%	2%	4%	5%	6%	8%	10%	12%	15%	19%	23%	28%	34%	41%
85%	2%	2%	4%	5%	6%	8%	9%	12%	15%	18%	22%	27%	32%	39%
80%	2%	2%	4%	5%	6%	7%	9%	11%	14%	17%	20%	25%	30%	37%
75%	2%	2%	3%	4%	5%	7%	8%	10%	13%	16%	19%	23%	28%	36%
70%	1%	2%	3%	4%	5%	6%	8%	10%	12%	15%	18%	22%	26%	32%
65%	1%	2%	3%	4%	5%	6%	7%	8%	11%	14%	17%	20%	25%	30%
60%	1%	2%	3%	4%	4%	5%	7%	8%	10%	13%	15%	19%	23%	28%
55%	1%	1%	2%	3%	4%	5%	6%	8%	9%	12%	14%	17%	21%	25%
50%	1%	1%	2%	3%	4%	4%	6%	7%	9%	10%	13%	16%	19%	23%
45%	1%	1%	2%	3%	3%	4%	5%	6%	8%	9%	12%	14%	17%	21%
40%	1%	1%	2%	2%	3%	4%	4%	6%	7%	8%	10%	12%	15%	18%
35%	1%	1%	2%	2%	3%	3%	4%	5%	6%	7%	9%	11%	13%	16%
30%	1%	1%	1%	2%	2%	3%	3%	4%	5%	6%	8%	9%	11%	14%
25%	1%	1%	1%	1%	2%	2%	3%	3%	4%	5%	6%	8%	10%	12%
20%	+%	1%	1%	1%	1%	2%	2%	3%	3%	4%	5%	6%	8%	10%
15%	+%	+%	1%	1%	1%	1%	2%	2%	3%	3%	4%	5%	6%	7%
10%	+%	+%	+%	1%	1%	1%	1%	2%	2%	3%	3%	4%	4%	5%
5%	+%	+%	+%	+%	+%	+%	1%	1%	1%	1%	1%	1%	2%	2%
0%	0%	0%	0%	0%	0%	0%	0%	0%	0%	0%	0%	0%	0%	0%

OUTDOOR TEMPERATURE

Fig. 8-3. Outdoor-Indoor Relative Humidity Conversion Chart.

A humidistat control may be included with the unit. It keeps the humidity automatically at a constant level in the house. In hard water areas, it is worthwhile to get a central humidifier unit that has excess water flow, constant bleed or some other method that reduces the concentration of the hardness minerals.

Another thing to be on the lookout for when buying a unit is whether it is the kind of unit you can install yourself. The only problem a competent do-it-yourselfer may run into is when it comes to the electrical phase of the operation. All other aspects are easy enough to do, but unless you have experience with electrical wiring, you should not tackle this phase yourself.

Do all the work, if you wish, except for the electrical installation. For this call in a licensed electrician.

INSTALLING CENTRAL SYSTEM HUMIDIFIERS

Generally, good quality central system humidifiers can be divided into either of two classes: 1. pre-wired, which is a do-it-yourself model; 2. non pre-wired, which requires that the unit be wired into a 110/120V line. Up to the point of wiring, each is handled more or less the same way, as follows:

1. Turn off the furnace and the home's main water valve.

Fig. 8-4. Cut out the area in the ductwork according to instructions issued by the manufacturer.

2. Select a location, in accordance with the manufacturer's suggestions, on the warm air plenum that is near a cold water line (Fig. 8-4).

3. Tape the kit's mounting template onto the duct.

4. Drill or punch out the holes specified by the template.

5. Using tin snips, cut out the area marked off on the plenum.

6. Remove the template and file down or cut off jagged edges to give a neat opening.

7. Mount of baffle plate, screwing it to the plenum with sheetmetal screws. Then mount the unit (Fig. 8-5).

8. Place the self-tapping saddle or compression nut on the water line and screw it down until it penetrates. If your home is equipped with a water softener, you should attempt to connect the humidifer to the regular water supply to avoid a buildup of sodium residue which softened water can deposit in the humidifier reservoir.

9. Connect the humidifier's water supply tubing from the cold water line to the unit (Fig. 8-6).

10. Wire the system. With a pre-wired model, this is done simply by hooking the plug-in transformer into a nearby

Fig. 8-5. Mount the unit in the cutout opening.

135

Fig. 8-6. Connect the water line by using the self-tapping compression valve included in the kit.

outlet. With a non pre-wired unit, you have to mount a junction box and wire the unit through the box to a 115V line.

11. Turn on the furnace and the main water valve. Set the water level control so water level is maintained ½ to 1 inch below the top of the reservoir.

It's important to keep your humidifier in good working order year in and year out. It must be thoroughly cleaned before and after the heating season, and periodically through the winter months. Follow the manufacture's instructions in the owner's manual that accompanies the unit.

Chapter 9
When You Should Consider a Heat Pump

When You Should Consider a Heat Pump

The heat pump was first introduced in a major way about 20 years ago. Today it is getting new attention because of its energy efficiency.

You can think of a heat pump as a furnace that also air conditions. Basically, an air conditioner works by moving warm air out of the house. A heat pump works that way, too, but in the winter reverses itself: it extracts heat from the air and routes it inside. Even in sub-zero weather, air contains heat which can be extracted.

When the heat pump first came out, it wasn't well accepted. Many fly-by-night outfits entered the market with inferior equipment and many companies—even good ones—didn't have the service organizations to care for the units. More important, it was discovered that the machines, which operated well in mild temperatures in the South, did not stand up well to the cold in the North. Today, however, heat pumps are made to withstand cold, and can be used in any area of the country. Also, service has improved markedly.

ECONOMIC ASPECTS

Installation of a typical heat pump costs up to 25% more than installation of a gas or oil furnace plus central air conditioning. It'll cost even more if the heat pump is replacing an electric furnace. Average cost of a heat pump is $1,500 to $1,700.

Heat pumps use a forced air distribution system. If the existing duct work does not require a great amount of modification, the job can be done for under $2,000. If duct work must be installed in an existing home or a new home, costs will range, on the average, from $4,000 to $5,000.

The above figures are for a so-called "split system" heat pump (Fig. 9-1). One machine is outside the house, and one inside. Piggyback heat pumps are also available. These install right on an existing furnace and work in tandem with the existing furnace to heat the home. As you might expect, they cost less.

The efficiency of a heat pump drops as outside temperatures go down. Heat pumps at this time can not work independently below

Fig. 9-1. Split system heat pump has one unit inside the house, one outside. Electric strip heaters on the inside unit take over when the temperature gets too low.

Fig. 9-2. Piggyback heat pump can be installed on existing furnace, like a central air conditioner.

28°F. At these low temperatures, the conventional furnace takes over if you have a piggyback unit, or electric strip heaters if you have a split system.

But, in general, heat pumps are more efficient than conventional heating plants, especially electric furnaces. In one test in the Southwest, a heat pump easily outperformed an electric furnace. The heat pump cost only $150 for a year versus $378 for the electric furnace, based on a rate of 2¢ per kilowatt hour. Heat pumps usually are not as efficient for cooling as central air conditioners. The best central air conditioners have an EER rate of about 11, while the top heat pumps are only a little over 8.

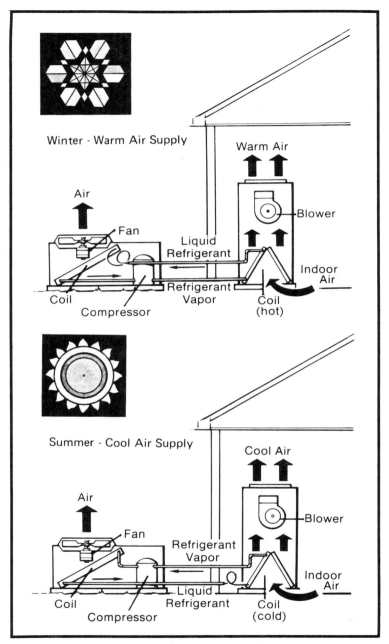

Fig. 9-3. How heat pumps work. Illustration on top shows winter operation; bottom illustration shows summer operation.

Before you purchase a heat pump, variables to consider include the climate you live in, the cost of installing the unit, cost of electricity cost of service and price of the heat pump itself. For example, if you could install a split system heat pump for $1,500, thereby eliminating a need for a furnace and central air conditioning, and the climate you lived in was relatively mild and fuel costs high, it might well be worth considering.

Another situation in which you might want to consider the installation of a heat pump would be if you have central air conditioning which requires replacement. Here, a piggyback heat pump could be used (Fig. 9-2). In some cases, it would do as good a job as central air, and it would always be there for use as a heating plant should fuel costs continue to increase. Also, if you plan air conditioning in the future, a piggyback heat pump could be used.

If you decide to buy a heat pump, check first with the large manufacturers, such as York, Carrier or Lennox. You can be reasonably sure that servicing will be available from these firms.

HOW A HEAT PUMP WORKS

For cooling, indoor air is drawn over the indoor unit's coil by the blower, cooling the air for recirculation throughout the home (Fig. 9-3). The liquid refrigerant in the coil is changed into a vapor as it absorbs the indoor heat. The refrigerant vapor is drawn into the compressor located in the outdoor unit, where its temperature and pressure are increased. The compressor then pumps the vapor into the outdoor coil where it is condensed into a liquid by action of fan-forced air flow over the coil. Before entering the indoor coil, where the cycle began, the refrigerant goes through a coiled capillary tube where its pressure is reduced, with a corresponding reduction in temperature.

For heating, the cycle is, in effect, reversed. Indoor air is drawn over the indoor unit's coil by the blower, warming the air for recirculation throughout the home. The hot refrigerant vapor in the coil is cooled and condensed to a high pressure liquid by this action. It then flows through a pressure-reducing capillary tube into the outdoor unit's coil where it picks up heat from outdoor air drawn over the coil by the fan. The compressor then increases the refrigerant's pressure and heat before pumping it into the indoor coil to complete the cycle.

Chapter 10
The Right Way to
Use Supplementary Heaters

The Right Way to Use Supplementary Heaters

There are times when a supplementary heating unit makes sense. For example, say you have a room that is not heated, but you want it heated for occasional use. Hooking this room into your existing heating system could be an expensive proposition. One answer is a supplementary heating unit.

Another situation is when your existing heating is inadequate to heat an addition. Rather than enlarge the system, a costly process, a supplementary unit could be used. There also are situations in which it simply would be impractical to extend the heating system to an area remote from your house.

ELECTRIC HEAT

Generally the most popular way among do-it-yourselfers to provide supplementary heating to an area is with electrical units. A big advantage is that they don't have to be vented. A possible disadvantage is operating cost.

Electricity can be expensive in certain areas of the country. Check the cost of operating the unit you plan to use with your utility company. Some units will also require individual circuits.

Baseboard heaters are a very popular type of unit (Fig. 10-1). These look just like baseboards, and usually have a liquid or resistance coils inside which give off the heat. Individual thermostats control the units. While baseboard heaters are geared to be installed

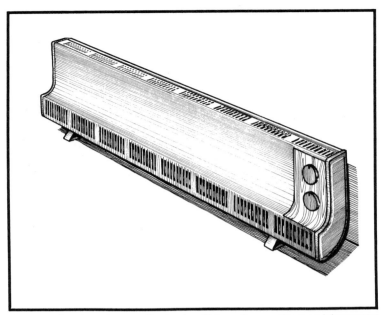

Fig. 10-1. Baseboard convection heater. Note wattage settings and thermostat controls.

on baseboards, there are also strip heaters which work essentially the same way but can be installed in floors, walls, ceilings and above doors.

RADIANT HEAT

Radiant heating panels are another source of supplemental heating. Heating panels using radiant energy are not new. They have been used for about 10 years, but have only recently become available to do-it-yourselfers (Fig. 10-2).

The panels have a surface composed of silicon crystals which disperse heat in all directions and can maintain a surface temperature of 200°. Panels come in 2′ × 4′ or 2′ × 2′ sizes and are mounted in T-bar ceiling arrangements or surface mounted on ceilings (Fig. 10-3) or walls (Fig. 10-4). The only requirements are access to a junction box for electrical hookup plus a means of fastening the frame to rafters or a slab ceiling.

Panels are effective on ceilings because radiant heat does not rise to the ceiling like hot air does. They work best when installed close to outside walls, particularly above windows or exterior doors.

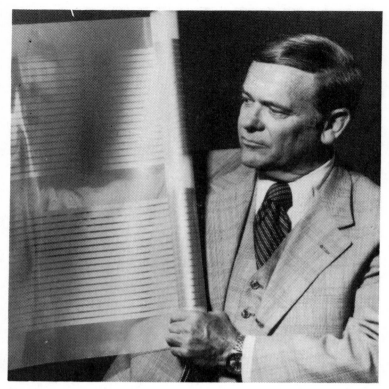
Fig. 10-2. Thermostatically controlled flexible radiant heating elements sealed in a plastic envelope offer another system of heating. By this—the ESWA system—sheets are rolled between ceiling joists, over sheetrock or plaster, before installing insulation.

When a thermostat is installed, it should be in the same room on an inside wall about 5′ above the floor.

Also available on the market are plug-in "picture" panels with silk screen designs for wall hanging. The largest (2′ × 3′) panels can supply heat for a 10′ × 15′ area using 500 watts of electricity. In small rooms or mobile homes, the picture panels can provide all the heat needed. They may be used in bathrooms or near swimming pools.

The panel's heating element is composed of two sheets of asbestos paper bound around a layer of graphite. An electrical current creates an even heat flow through the asbestos. The asbestos is insulated by a layer of fiberglass, which is in turn encased in a steel panel. The front of the panel is coated with epoxy, then sprinkled with fine sand. The sand is held in place by two layers of latex paint, enabling the panel front to be washed or repainted.

Other types of radiant heaters may be used portably (moved from spot to spot), hung from a wall or suspended from the ceiling. They range from about 2,000 watts up to 6,000 watts. This type has a heavy duty electric element that generates a great deal of heat which is blown into an area by a built-in fan (Fig. 10-5). You can either plug the heater in an outlet or wire it permanently into house wiring.

Many radiant heaters have swivel bases that allow you to direct the heat in various direction. Such units should have a positive lock to insure that the heater remains as positioned.

Electric space heaters which depend on the convection of air are also available. These have no moving parts and never get hot enough to be hazardous, as many radiant heaters do. Still, they do a good heating job. According to one manufacturer, a convection heater "will maintain a 3° differential between floor and ceiling temperatures" and will "give a desired level of comfort at lower energy input than any radiant heater."

Typically the heating unit of this type heater consists of a large number of aluminum fins shaped to emit a rising steam of warm air.

Fig. 10-3. Radiant heating panels such as the Aztec unit shown here may be installed on walls or ceilings and are often used in kitchens, bathrooms and workshops.

147

Note: New Emerson-Chromalox AWH series architectural wall heaters are available in two versions to meet residential, commercial and institutional application needs. The AWH 2000 version (right) is designed for deluxe residential and commercial installations. The AWH 5000 version is a heavy-duty unit with 16-gauge grille and tamperproof control, for commercial and institutional applications. Models are available in both versions to provide 1500 – 4000 watts output at 208, 240, 277 volts. For further information, write to Emerson-Chromalox Division, Emerson Electric Co., Station 2927, 8100 West Florissant Avenue, St. Louis, Missouri 63136.

Fig. 10-4. Wall-mounted electric heaters, such as this Emerson-Chromalox unit, may be installed wherever you can run electric cable.

The unit draws in cold air from the floor, sends it through the heated aluminum fins and converts it to rising warm air.

Convection heaters weigh from 10 to 15 lbs. Those with large heat output, such as for use in an unheated garage, are rated at 1,500 watts, but you can also buy units rated at 5,000 watts and up. Ideally, an electric heater should have a wattage control to allow you to adjust electrical input to an energy-conserving level. A heater can also be thermostatically controlled.

INFRARED HEAT

Another type of heater is the infrared. This type uses quartz lamps which are energized by electricity. The lamps emit electromagnetic wave lengths which are absorbed by people and objects beneath the fixture, which is mounted on the ceiling. Heat coverage is limited to the area directly beneath the unit.

FUEL-TYPE HEATERS

Heaters that burn oil or kerosene can also be used for supplementary heating. One type is a window-mounted furnace (Fig. 10-6) that uses ordinary kerosene or No. 1 fuel oil and, according to its manufacturer, "delivers 39,000 Btu of clean heat at one-third the cost of electric space-heating." The 108-lb. unit slides into an opening that is a minimum 25″ wide by 14½″ high, just about the size required by a window air conditioner. It has a built-in 5-gal. fuel tank. Fuel ignition is provided by a standard electric outlet.

Fig. 10-5. Typical radiant space heater. Heavy duty electric element generates heat transferred by built-in fan.

Fig. 10-6. This Koehring window-mounted furnace resembles a window air conditioner. It uses kerosene or No. 1 fuel oil and has a 5-gallon fuel tank.

Portable space heaters that use No. 1 fuel oil are also available (Fig. 10-7). They weigh about 35 lbs, and may be shifted from one part of a room to another as required. They generate enough heat to warm a space with a volume of about 5,000 cu. ft. Some of these space heaters have built-in thermostats; on other models the thermostat is optional.

The units run off standard household current and require less electricity to operate than a 300-watt bulb. The electricity is used to ignite fuel and operate the motor that blows out the heat. The price generally runs from $150 to $300.

WOOD HEATERS

You can buy small wood-burning heaters, or buy door/draft control fittings that can be attached to a 30-gal. drum. You can then burn scrap wood from the shop, rolled newspapers or cordwood to heat the shop. Before buying or installing a wood-burning unit, check local building codes for safety requirements regarding chimney and draft specifications. As a general guide, no temporary heating unit should be left unattended. Fire codes normally forbid use of any non-permanent heater for overnight heating.

SAFETY FIRST

No matter what type of heater you decide to use, there are several very important safety guidelines that should be observed.

Think of safety first and watch out for supplementary heater hazards.
Permanently installed heating equipment usually has fewer hazards
because it is more out of the way. Supplementary heaters have some
special problems that all members of the family must recognize.

- Provide barriers or locate floor units out of normal paths
  through rooms to prevent tripping.
- Provide barriers to high surface temperatures and maintain
  clearance to combustibles.
- Provide adequate ventilation for fuel-type heaters. These
  units need combustion air venting.
- Never service your heater when the power cord is plugged
  in.
- Before using the heater for the first time at the start of the
  heating season, check it for obstructions. If the system uses
  fuel, see that there are no leaks. Check the electric cord for
  deterioration and damage.
- Never use a heater unless you provide adequate ventilation.
  Generally, a minimum of 1½ sq. ft. of ventilating area is

Fig. 10-7. Portable fuel space heaters, which burn No. 1 fuel oil, may be used if
an electric outlet is available.

151

adequate. This is equivalent to the opening formed when a 16-foot-long garage door is raised 1 inch from the ground.

- Never use a portable, fueled space heater in sleeping quarters.
- Make certain there are no combustible or flammable materials around, such as fresh paint, fuel and cleaning solvents.
- When moving a heater from one spot to another, disconnect the power cord. Always plug the heater into a grounded circuit.
- If you have a heater that uses kerosene or No. 1 fuel oil, don't fill the tank while the heater is operating.
- Keep a portable dry chemical fire extinguisher on hand just in case.

Chapter 11
How to Get More
from Appliance Energy

How to Get More from Appliance Energy

Proper use of appliances can also help to cut energy bills. Total consumer energy use includes 10.2% for space heating, 2.3% for water heating and 2% for all major appliance applications. Other home uses are lighting, 0.3%; television, 0.3% and all small appliances 0.1%.

In this chapter, you'll see how you can cut energy needs by the wise purchase and use of applicances.

New electronic devices called the microprocessors are available to replace electro-mechanical and solid-state controls on new washers and dryers, as well as dishwashers and microwave ovens. (A microprocessor, smaller than a dime, is a set of silicon chips that accepts inputs, produces pre-determined outputs to operate a product and is programmable.)

New appliances with microprocessors and related electronic control devices are available for only about $10 to $20 more than conventional models. They have the potential of trimming your utility bills if your utility has some kind of off-peak rate reduction, and you schedule appliance use during non-peak periods. The new controls also help match water levels and appliance cycles more accurately to your needs.

REFRIGERATORS/FREEZERS

Food refrigeration ranks behind heating and water heating but slightly ahead of air conditioning in home energy uses. New refrigeratiors and freezers also tout energy saving features (Fig. 11-5), but the first consideration is to make sure you get the right size for your family. The following appliances (Figs. 11-1 through 11-4) from Sears offer the benefits of microprocessors. The Lady Kenmore washer, with solid state controls, has an electronic control panel which allows nearly an unlimited number of control modes to match home laundry needs. The Kenmore dishwasher, dryer, and microwave oven offer similar solid-state controls; have no gears or other moving control parts to wear out.

Refrigerators range in capacity from 1.7 to 27.8 cubic feet; freezers range from 4.5 to 31.1 cubic feet. An important factor in

Fig. 11-1. New Lady Kenmore washer features solid-state controls. A touch of a finger on the electronic control panel can program the appliance to perform any one of 12 different wash functions. By using various combinations, consumers can select a nearly unlimited number of different control modes to meet their home laundry needs. Washer continues to feature exclusive Dual-Action agitator which provides for uniform cleaning of large loads.

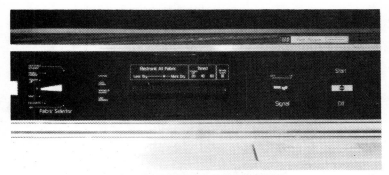

Fig. 11-2. A touch of a finger to the cycle selector pad programs new Kenmore dishwasher—first with solid-state controls. With electronic control system, there are no mechanical gears or other moving control parts to wear out. Lighted control panel shows cycle and options selected as well as phase of cycle when in operation.

choosing refrigerator and freezer capacity is the waste of energy involved in too frequent shopping trips if you do not have enough space to accommodate your refrigerated and frozen food needs.

While it is impossible here to evaluate all the refrigerators and freezers on the market, here are some general guidelines that will help you select an energy-efficient unit.

Frost-free models generally require more electricity to operate than manual-defrost units. Manual defrosting is a messy job, but will save you energy.

Manual defrost refrigerators are only available in relatively small capacities. The largest available manual defrost refrigerators (approximately 13 cu. ft. capacity) use from 40 to 70 kilowatt hours per month. Partially automatic (refrigerator only) defrost models use from 50 to 110 kWh in the same approximate capacity category. Fully automatic models range from 87 to 157 kWh.

The differences are even less, of course, on smaller units. Automatic defrosting freezers are offered only in larger upright-type units (over 10 cu. ft.).

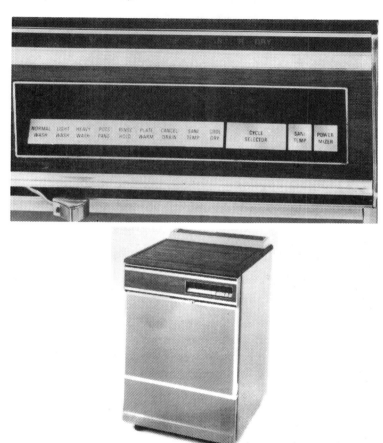

Fig. 11-3. New Lady Kenmore solid-state dryer offers consumers simplified and meaningful controls. The Fabric Selector on the left allows for seven temperature levels, from the hottest for cotton and sturdy fabrics to the lowest settings for delicate fabrics and air only. The All Fabric control in the center allows the consumer to select the amount of moisture allowed to remain in the clothes. Through the use of a microprocessor, the All Fabric control insures uniform dryness, regardless of the fabric, time after time when the same settings are used.

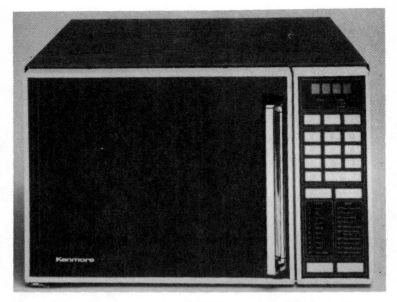

Fig. 11-4. New Kenmore large-capacity microwave oven features multi-power cooking control, temperature sensing probe, time-of-day clock and memory. Touch of finger can program solid-state oven to memorize two sets of time and power-level instructions. It also contains "hold/warm" feature.

Ask the dealer to tell you how many kilowatts each unit uses per month. All new appliances will have annual energy cost information on labels. You can use this data to evaluate the efficiency of one model versus another. The annual cost-of-energy figure is the final answer for comparing since it takes into account the interaction of factors such as motor efficiency and insulation.

Check to see if the unit uses electric heater strips around the doors to eliminate condensation on the outside of the door during periods of high humidity. Newest energy-efficient units are provided with a switch which can turn off these strips when the humidity is low. Some models don't use strips but circulate around the door some of the heat developed by the refrigeration system. No shut-off switch is provided or needed for these types.

A multi-doored freezer or refrigerator will let in less room heat than a single door model.

A chest freezer is more efficient than an upright model because the cold air settles on the bottom and isn't lost when the lid is lifted. However proper use is important too. Energy may be wasted if you must hold the chest freezer door open for a long time while you rummage through the unit for frozen food packages.

When using a refrigerator or freezer, check to see if you can save more energy by following these practices:

- Keep the temperature adjusted properly. There are many variables. Refrigerated foods should be kept cool but not frozen. Temperature may vary in different parts of the unit. Temperature in freezer should not exceed 10°F. Consistency of ice cream is a good guide.
- Try to limit the number of times a unit's door is opened. Keep the door open only briefly.

Fig. 11-5. This 19-cu. ft. Whirlpool refrigerator/freezer has a power-saving heater control switch for use when room humidity is low. Insulation advances allow thinwall construction.

- Cover moisture-laden food. The moisture is drawn into the air and the unit has to work harder. Don't quick chill warm food unless a recipe calls for it. Let the food cool gradually, then place in the refrigerator. About 20 minutes of pre-cooling is safe—otherwise bacteria growth can start.

You also can stretch energy dollars by keeping refrigerators and freezers properly maintained. This checklist outlines what you can do:

- A refrigerator should be level. Most have feet that can be adjusted for leveling. Some manufacturers recommend that the unit be adjusted with a slight backward tilt so that the door will close by itself.
  With a manual defrost unit, defrost it before the frost becomes ¼" thick. Excess frost makes the compressor work extra hard and wastes energy.
- Make sure door seals are tight. Gaskets on present-day refrigerators or freezers seldom wear out or deteriorate as older rubber types used to. Mis-alignment of doors is rare unless the door has been damaged or abused. Damaged gaskets on older units should be checked, and replaced if necessary. A much more common and serious energy waste occurs if you neglect to fully close the refrigerator or freezer door or if items inside hold it slightly open.
- Keep the condenser coils clean and clear of obstructions, as well as the grill on the front of the unit near the bottom. Use a vacuum very carefully from time to time.
- Regular cleaning is important. This eliminates the need for re-refrigerationg foods removed during major cleaning. Manual defrost models must, of course, be defrosted; this means that additional energy must be used to re-refrigerate and re-freeze foods removed for defrosting.

Also make sure you use food items in the refrigerator and freezer before you have to throw them out. All the energy used in storing them, and the food itself, are wasted when this happens.

RANGES AND OVENS

As with refrigerators, there are many energy saving features to consider in buying a range (Fig. 11-6) or oven. One feature is an electronically lighted pilot available on gas ranges. No gas burns until you turn these on; you save up to 30% on gas use.

When using any range, here are some good energy-saving practices to follow:

- Top burners provide the most efficient heat transfer. Use them whenever possible.
- In electric cooking surface elements may be turned off before the food is done, as burners should be shut off as

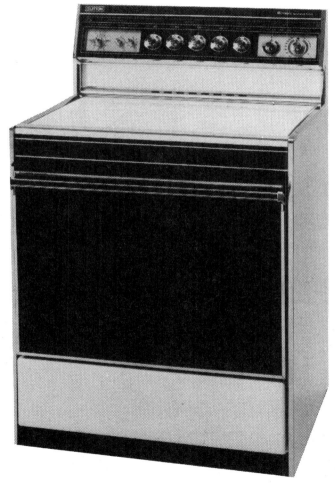

Fig. 11-6. This Litton range combines a conventional oven with the energy-saving features of a microwave.

soon as you are through using them. Forgetting to turn off surface elements is highly wasteful.

- If there are reflector pans below the burners, keep these clean. These help focus heat on utensil bottoms.
- Use pots and pans that fit burner size. A pot or pan should never be larger than 1″ all around the burner; nor should it be smaller. Too small and heat will escape. Too large and the heat at the center of the pan and the outer rim of the burner will be uneven.
- If possible, use pans and pots with flat bottoms and straight sides and make sure covers are tightly sealed. Follow the recipe for cooking time and temperature.

OVENS

When selecting an oven, you find you can buy either continuous-cleaning or self-cleaning ovens. The continuous-cleaning version uses less energy. A self-cleaning oven, on the average, takes about 3 kilowatt hours to clean an electric oven; a gas oven takes about 0.5 therm (1 therm equals 100,000 Btu).

There are ways you can save energy when using either a range or oven:

If you have a choice of cooking something on the surface units of the range or in the oven, use the surface units. They are 8 to 10 times more efficient than ovens.

- If oven shelves have to be rearranged, do this before the oven is turned on. Doing it while it's on lets heat escape, wastes energy, risks burned fingers and ignition of pot holders.
- Try to keep peeking into the oven to a minimum. If oven is properly cared for and timer and controls are accurate you have little need to peek.
- When using dishes made of ceramic, glass and stainless steel it's possible to lower an oven some 25°F.
- When browning foods, do this on medium-high settings, then reduce the setting for finishing the job.

DISHWASHERS

There are a variety of energy saving features you can get when buying a dishwasher. These include partial load cycles, rinse-only cycles, and mid-cycle turnoff. Look for a quality, well-insulated machine and a cushioned pump. Following are ways you can get more work from dishwashers per energy dollar:

- Don't pre-rinse with running water.
- Use the shortest cycle available for washing dishes.
- Follow the manufacturer's directions when loading the machine.

Don't use ordinary detergent in a dishwasher. Use only detergent expressly designed for machines. Regular detergent can cause excessive sudsing, cut down washing action and create other problems.

- Wash dishes when dishwasher is filled to capacity.
- You can air-dry dishes without the use of heat with virtually all dishwashers. Simply open the door. Some new models have a switch which permits the user to shut off the hot air during the drying cycle.

LAUNDRY EQUIPMENT

Washing machines and dryers are two other major appliances you can save on (Fig. 11-7). Again, buy a machine that is sized for your needs. In reference to the purchase of a washer, a larger unit may be the best buy. It is more energy efficient to do one large load of washing than it is to do two or three small loads.

Here are tips to save energy with washing machines:

- Fill the machine with clothes to its capacity before using it. The washer will require just as much energy to do one item as it would to do a large load.
- Don't use excessive amounts of detergent. This interferes with washing action and two rinses instead of one may be required to clear out the detergent.
- Presoak treatment can help remove stubborn stains or unusual soil. This can help eliminate the need for washing the clothes a second time.
- Carefully follow the laundering instructions on the garment. If it suggests cold water washing and rinsing use cold water; if it suggests a hot wash and warm rinse follow this advice, etc.
- Use cycles appropriate to the job to be done. For dryers try these energy-saving tips:
- Use the short cycle on the dryer whenever possible.

Fig. 11-7. This GE washer features "Mini-Basket" and "Mini-Quick" cycle for small loads or delicate items.

- If you have more than one load to dry, do it right after the first. This way the dryer will be close to operating temperature.
- Keep vents and the lint filter clean. Clean the lint filter after each use to insure a free flow of air and more efficient drying.
- Don't over-dry clothes. This not only wastes energy, but can also make clothes feel stiff. Experimentation is the only answer. It's also helpful to dry items of the same material together. Dry heavy and light items separately. This way the dryer heat won't go to waste on items in the tumbler that are already dry.

SAVING HOT WATER

It's a fact that a leaky hot water faucet wastes energy to an incredible degree. It is estimated that a faucet that leaks a drop a second will waste 2,400 gallons of water a year. To put that in perspective, that amount of water would flush a toilet 480 times or do 160 loads of wash. Another fact is that, on the average, the energy used to heat water represents about 15% of a total energy bill.

First, make sure that your water heater is sized to your family's needs. The American Gas Association provides some guidelines on how big a unit should be. A family with two people using one bath and a washing machine should have a water heater with a 30 gal. capacity. For another bath and every other person add 3½ gal. If a dishwasher is used, add an additional 5 gal. capacity.

If your water heater has seen better days, and you plan to replace it, check the operating efficiency of new units. The tank should also be well insulated; better quality tanks are glass-lined. If gas, check for an energy conserving pilot light. And, if practical, position the heater as close to the point of use as possible.

HEATER USE

Set the thermostat on a water heater to only the levels you need. A rule of thumb is that if you have a dishwasher, 140°F is right. If you don't have a dishwasher, water will be hot enough at 110° to 120°F. But there are exceptions:

You will probably need water that is hotter than 140°F if you wash heavily soiled items (e.g., work clothes, diapers) or if control of infections is needed. Also the temperatures cited may be okay unless the water flows for a considerable distance from the water heater to the points of use through uninsulated water pipes. Wrap pipes with an insulating material.

In colder areas with 35°F water delivered in winter, the thermostat has to be set at 135°F minimum unless it is just for hand washing. A shower in the morning from a "medium" insulated tank will usually deliver 110°F hot water at first, then cool down below 90°F due to a wide thermostat differential of up to 25°F.

If your utility company offers lower rates for using hot water in off-peak hours (usually in early morning and midevening), take advantage of it. Some water heaters come with two heating elements. One element can be used to heat a small amount of water, say 20 gal., during peak usage, and a large amount of water during off-peak hours.

Also, if you find that your hot water has to travel long distances be sure pipes are wrapped. Or, you can use the tank near the dishwasher and set the thermostat at 140°F. This lets you set the main thermostat at 110° to 120°F. This lower temperature setting will help you recoup the cost of the tank.

WATER HEATER CARE

Like any appliance, a water heater requires regular maintenance. Every month draw about five gallons from the tank to flush away mineral deposits in the water. Left alone, these deposits can build up a hard crust that insulates the heat source from the water.

Chapter 2 shows how to insulate a tank to save energy. If your tank feels warm to the touch, it should be insulated. In severe cases, where heaters are subject to extreme cold, wrapping the tank with insulation can help even more. Here are other tips:

- Take showers instead of baths. You'll use less hot water.
- Don't let water run while you shave.
- If you plan to be away from home for extended periods, dial the thermostat down to the lowest setting.
- Use a flow control device on showers. It can almost cut water use in half.
- Using smaller appliances whenever you can is a wise energy-saving step. Savings are generally possible with small appliances if *small* quantities are involved and if the appliance is used for the purpose intended.

SAVING ON LIGHTING

On the average, lighting accounts for around 3½% of the energy used in a home and up to 16% of the entire cost of electricity. One good way to save on lighting is to use the right bulbs.

The most common kind of bulb is the incandescent, which has a life expectancy of up to 1,000 hours. While long-life bulbs will last up to 2,500 hours, they yield about 20% less light per watt. It doesn't pay to use them except in places such as stairways where replacement is difficult.

Also available are bulbs filled with krypton gas. They have a lower wattage than standard bulbs out produce the same light and will last up to 600 hours longer. If you have a choice, always use an incandescent bulb with a high wattage rather than a low wattage. One 100-watt bulb will produce about the same amount of light as two 60-watt bulbs, but uses about 20% less power.

FLUORESCENTS

The best energy savers among bulbs are fluorescents. They give off three to five times more light than incandescent bulbs, and last up to 10 times longer. For example, a 40-watt fluorescent will produce 3200 lumens (a measurement of light) while a 100-watt incandescent only 1750.

You can cut energy costs by using new efficient fluorescent lighting units and adapters.

One new fixture available converts an incandescent lamp or fixture into a fluorescent to save you about 50% on your light bill with

Fig. 11-8. "Killer Watt" is an adapter that converts an incandescent lamp into a fluorescent light which will last 12 times as long, burn cooler, and save 50% on light bills. By Johnson Industries.

Fig. 11-9. GE's Bright Stik is a 25″ fluorescent lighting unit that produces as much light as a 50-watt incandescent bulb, and lasts five times as long.

no loss in light intensity. The adapter screws into any standard socket of a lamp or fixture already in the home. Using standard circline bulbs, the device is available in single and double units, depending on the wattage desired (Fig. 11-8).

Because it burns cooler, it can save on home air conditioning costs. It also procuces less glare and shadow than incandescent lamps. The small fluorescent unit has the same low-maintenance and energy-saving qualities of larger commercial units.

Another new fluorescent lighting unit worth considering is called the Bright Stik by General Electric (Fig. 11-9). It weighs only 9 oz., lasts five times as long and produces as much light as a 50-watt incandescent bulb. The unit comes ready to plug in and turn on wherever light is needed. Service life, according to G.E., is three to five years under normal use. The 25″ unit comes with a 6′ cord which houses the on-off switch.

The potential savings of converting to fluorescent lighting on a national basis is dramatic. An average of 600 billion kilowatt hours of electricity is used in the U.S. per year. If homes were fully converted to fluorescent lighting the total savings would be 150 billion kilowatt hours per year, or $5,250,000,000 at 3½¢ per kilowatt hour.

BULB PLACEMENT

Using light efficiently also involves positioning fixtures right. For example, for a desk in room, workbench or kitchen counter, you can provide spot lighting over these specific areas and get by with less general lighting. The same can be done in recreation or family rooms where only spot lighting is usually required. If fixtures are in a few locations, you can control the lighting and save money.

Another way to save is to control lights by dimmer switches. The lower the lights, the more power you will save. The same thing is true for 3-way bulbs.

What about turning lights on and off frequently to save energy? Which is better? It depends. If you plan to leave a room for more than three minutes, turn the light off if it's an incandescent type. If a fluorescent, turn it off if you'll be leaving for more than 15 minutes. Turning off lights more frequently than this can lead to burning them out more quickly.

Lighting timers can also be useful in saving energy. Use them outside the house for turning lights on and off, as needed, rather than leaving them on all the time. The same thing applies to inside lights. Have them hooked up to a timer when you'll be away from the home for extended periods.

All lights should be kept clean. You'll be surprised at how much more efficient a light is when clean.

Also use natural light. Trim shrubbery that blocks light coming in windows. During cold weather, have drapes open during the day to allow light, as well as heat, to enter the home. Light colored materials also help. Shades with white liners reflect more light. If possible, set lights so the bottom of the shade is at eye level and about 40″ from the floor. Hanging lights, ideally, should be set up in corners so they can reflect off light colored walls.

BE AN ENERGY-EFFICIENT BUYER

An appliance labeling program to help consumers shop for energy-saving household appliances and equipment is being developed by the Federal Energy Administration and the Federal Trade Commission as a result of the Energy Policy and Conservation Act signed into law on December 22, 1975.

Under the law, manufacturers must place labels showing estimated annual operating costs on all models of central air-conditioners, clothes dryers, clothes washers, dishwashers, freezers, furnaces, home heating equipment (not including furnaces), humidifiers and dehumidifiers, kitchen ranges and ovens, refrigerators and refrigerator-freezers, room air conditioners, television sets, and water heaters.

Appliance testing, labeling and public information procedures are still being developed. For current information on this program, write the Federal Energy Administration, Appliance Program, Washington, D.C. 20461.

Power Consumption Of Household Appliances

Appliance	Average Wattage	Estimated kWh Consumed Annually
Food Preservation	341	1,195
Food freezer (15 cu ft)	250	750
Refrigerator	325	1,150
Refrigerator-freezer (14 cu ft)	350	1,400
Refrigerator-freezer (frostless 14 cu ft)		
Climate Control		
Air conditioner (room)	1,400	595
Dehumidifier	257	377
Fan (attic)	370	291
Fan (circuilating)	88	43
Fan (furnace)	282	394
Fan (roll-about)	171	138
Heat lamp (infrared)	250	13
Heat pump	11,848	16,003
Heater (radiant)	1,322	176
Humidifier	177	163
Oil burner or stoker	266	410
Resistance heaters	15,000	17,000
Air conditioner (central)	5,000	2,500
Food Preparation		
Broiler	1,140	85
Carving knife	95	0.8
Coffee maker	600	138
Deep-fat fryer	1,448	83
Dishwasher	800	242
Food blender	300	0.9
Food mixer (hand)	80	1
Food waste disposer	445	30
Frying pan	1,200	100
Grill (sandwich/waffle iron)	1,200	25
Hot plate	1,257	90
Range	1,220	1,175
Roaster	1,425	60
Toaster	1,100	39
Waffle iron	1,116	22

continued on page 171

continued from page 170

Appliance	Average Wattage	Estimated kWh Consumed Annually
Home Entertainment	71	86
Radio-phonograph	237	262
Television (black and white)	332	375
Television (color)		
Laundry	4,856	993
Clothes dryer	1,100	60
Iron (hand)	260	78
Washing machine (automatic)	195	59
Washing machine (nonautomatic)		
Appliance		
Water Heaters	4,474	4,219
Miscellaneous		
Clock	2.5	22
Floor polisher	305	15
Hair dryer	400 to 900	25 to 45
Heating pad	60	3
Sewing machine	75	11
Shaver	15	0.5
Sun lamp	279	16
Toothbrush	1	10
Vacuum cleaner	630	46
Bed covering	150	150

Sources: New York State Cooperative Extension Service and Association of Home Appliance Manufacturers. Note: These are average figures, your own comsumption totals and appliance operating costs may vary widely according to individual use and local utility rates.

Chapter 12
Ways to use
Wood to Cut Fuel Bills

Ways to use Wood to Cut Fuel Bills

Over the past few years homeowners across America have turned to woodburning fireplaces, stoves and furnaces as ways to cut down on fuel costs.

Manufacturers have responded to the rush to woodburners with a wide array of wood burning units. These can, if properly installed and operated, supplement home heat, and in some cases provide the bulk of the heat required by your home.

UPDATING FIREPLACES

You can update an existing masonry fireplace to make it more efficient. Chapter 13 shows you how to install a newer zero-tolerance prefab fireplace yourself. In either case, you should first understand the drawbacks of fireplaces which must be overcome to make fireplaces efficient heaters.

An existing fireplace of conventional design can actually increase, rather than decrease, fuel costs. There are a couple of reasons. First, a fire is a form of radiant heat—you might compare its pattern of heat to that of the light from a flashlight. Only some of the heat generated is radiated into a room. With conventional fireplaces most of the heat, about 85%, goes up the flue.

Second, a fire requires oxygen to burn. Conventional fireplaces draw heated air from inside a room. The air which has been warmed by your conventional heating plant is gobbled up by the fire and your furnace has to work harder. For example, assume that your chimney can exhaust 12,000 cu. ft. of air an hour. Assume your house is 1,200 sq. ft. and has normal 8' ceilings, for a total of 9,600 cu. ft. That means that the air in your house (9,600 cu. ft.) will turn over every hour.

A conventional fireplace will be less costly to operate in a totally unheated area isolated from the rest of the house in a room addition or porch. But usually, to get conventional fireplaces to pay off, you need to equip them with heat saving devices.

Heat recovery units for fireplaces are available in a wide assortment of designs to push heat from wood burned in the fireplace into your home. The cheapest to buy, and easiest to install, are special hollow-core replacement grates (Fig. 12-1). Some manufacturers say one of these units by itself can double the heat output of the fireplace.

Many commercially available replacement grates take advantage of natural convection. Cold air drawn into the opening of the hollow grate is heated at the bottom by the fire and forced out the top.

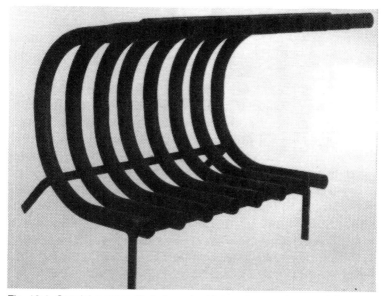

Fig. 12-1. Special grates with hollow steel tubes draw cool room air in at the bottom. Air is heated by fire and forced out into living area. Source: Fireplace Grate Heat Co.

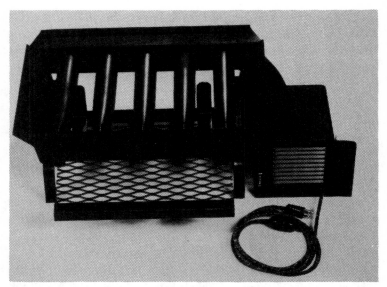

Fig. 12-2. Heat transfer units with blowers are available as replacement grates and other configurations. Some claim units help fireplaces give out five times more heat. Source: Marlin Metalcraft.

Forced air grate systems which use the same principle, but help nature along with mechanical blowers, are the next step up. Installing units with blowers often involves more than simply taking the old grate out and replacing it with one designed to save energy. However, companies producing such units say units with blowers can boost heat production five times over units without blowers.

Blower attachments designed to attach directly to separate tube-shaped grates are also available from manufacturers. Unitized grate systems which incorporate mechanical airflow into grate design are also available. Some units have two high-speed blowers which move about 160 cu. ft. of heated air per minute.

Manufacturers note that blower units (Fig. 12-2) have an additional advantage. Because the blowers transfer more air, the grate structure remains at a much cooler temperature, and will last years longer under normal use. Blowers also allow better distribution of heated air. For even better heat distribution, you can turn on the forced air fan in your existing furnace system (leaving flame off).

Some replacement grate heat recovery units are available with either front screen or glass doors. Glass doors can double the heat output of a blower unit up to 10,000 Btu's per hour.

176

Mechanized fireplace heat recovery units (Fig. 12-3), however, do not all employ the C-shaped grate design. Some use square tube heat exchanges which mount inside your fireplace at the top. Installation takes less than a half hour with two self-tapping screws or quick mount clamps. Fireplace screening or glass doors, again, can be added.

Got hot water baseboard heating? Grate-type heat recovery units which hook into your closed hot water system are also available. One unit generates up to 40,000 Btu's per hour. Some C-shaped grates also may be connected to either an existing boiler (hot water circulates into boiler, then throughout the house) or ducts of a forced air system.

Another good way you can update your fireplace is to install special fireboxes inside your conventional fireplace (Fig. 12-4). These allow for space between the firebox and interior of your fireplace. Cool air enters the space between the bottom of the box and the fireplace, is heated, and is forced out into the room by convection. Firebox inserts also incorporate glass doors. Advantage is that heated air in the room is reheated and returned to the room. The smaller amount of combustion air needed is regulated by special dampers at the front of the unit.

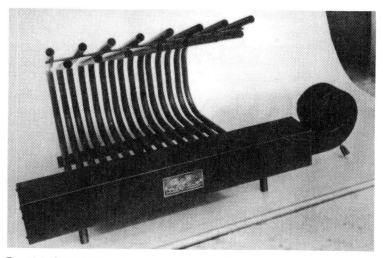

Fig. 12-3. Some heat exchange units, such as this one, are available as ready-to-assemble kits to salvage hot air which otherwise would go up the chimney. Source: Eagle Industries.

177

Fig. 12-4. Special convector firebox insert for conventional masonry fireplace can cut heat loss dramatically. Unit has its own special damper and is fitted with two glass doors. Source: El Fuego Corp.

A relatively simple way to extract more heat from your fireplace is to replace screening with glass doors. Glass doors earn back their cost fast since controlled intake draft reduces wood consumption and also offers safety from flying sparks. Glass fireplace doors are available with heat tempered glass (Fig. 12-5) in a choice of finishes, including baked-on enamel, flat black or polished and antique brass. The units, available in a wide assortment of sizes, come with glass wool insulation around the edges to ensure a tight fit to brick or other facing.

USING WOOD STOVES

The rising cost of energy has resulted in a rush to wood burning stoves (Fig. 12-6) both old and new. A wide variety of wood stoves (Fig. 12-7) for heating and cooking can be found on the market today, though operating principles boil down to about a half dozen. Study the market carefully before buying, and generally put most trust in the older, well-established firms.

The National Fire Protection Association recommends that if your wood stove is second-hand, you should check it over for cracks or defects such as faulty legs, hinges or draft louvers. Repair small cracks with stove cement, and have large cracks welded by an expert. New stoves should be of sturdy materials like cast iron.

WOOD-BURNING FURNACES

Wood burning units (see Chap. 14) which attach to your present furnace (Fig. 12-8) are available from a number of manufacturers. Or you can buy multi-fuel furnaces which allow you to use wood as well as conventional heating fuels. When wood burns down, the furnace switches to gas or oil Some multi-fuel furnaces even start wood fires automatically.

Multi-fuel furnaces (Fig. 12-9) cost more than conventional furnaces, and in some areas may not be accepted by local codes. They are available in warm air or boiler-type models. When buying a multi-fuel furnace, spend enough time to make sure you get a unit properly sized for your home, and study its efficiency rating. Check the length of logs it takes (longer logs mean less cutting), how ashes are removed, and if the unit will accept a humidifier or air conditioner. Some units are designed to run well only on wood; others not.

Do-it-yourself installation of these units is possible. But be sure to have the installed unit checked by heating specialists. Wood-

Fig. 12-5. Glass fireplace enclosures not only help conserve energy but also allow better control of burning speed and efficiency than conventional fireplace screens. Source: Bennett-Ireland.

Fig. 12-6. Wood stoves using a half-dozen operating designs are available in a variety of designs. The Jotul, a Scandinavian stove, uses a baffle and smoke chamber for increased heat efficiency. Source: Jotul.

burning furnaces may require more air than average oil or gas furnaces. If your home is well built and weather-tight you may need to provide extra air by installing a vent to the outdoors.

Whatever unit you decide to use, some important guidelines should be observed. Provide venting and use safe chimneys. A fireplace or stove, to burn coal, must have grates. Also provide for adequate clearances from combustible materials (Fig. 12-10). Following are other checks to make sure your woodstove or fireplace operates safely:

- Creosote build-up, when ignited, causes extremely hot fires. Scrape away accumulated creosote from the chimney with flat metal blade on a long handle. Don't damage mortar.
- Inspect, clean and repair chimneys every year before the heating season.

Fig. 12-7. The Shenandoah is a circulating heater and uses either wood or coal. Source: Shenandoah.

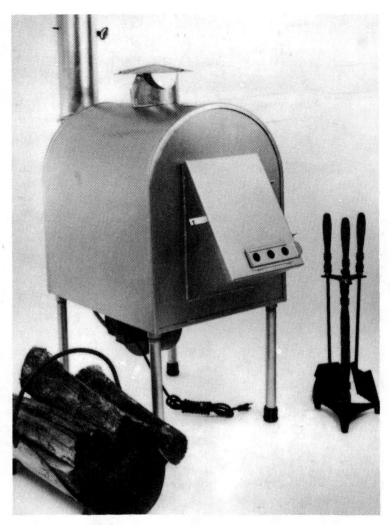

Fig. 12-8. The Silver Star unit has a blower and can be attached to existing furnaces. Source: Silver Star.

- If your chimney catches afire, don't pour water into it. Such an act could crack the flue liner or bricks. Call the fire department, dump lots of coarse salt on the fire and try putting out the fire. If you have a fireplace, hold a wet blanket over the hearth opening to keep air from entering the chimney.

Maintain heating equipment as recommended by the manufacturer. Overfiring (too much fuel) causes overheating; smoldering fuel produces accumulations of volatile residues. Using flammable liquids to start or rekindle fires causes flashovers. Defective equipment results in hot gases escaping.

GETTING WOOD

Many wood-burning units can either supplement your home furnace output or heat an entire lake cabin or other vacation retreat. This can be a decided advantage if your retreat is far from conventional heat sources such as gas lines or oil suppliers. If you can hustle the wood yourself from nearby woods, it'll cost you nothing. And if you cut your own wood, it'll warm you twice—once when you cut it, again when you burn it. If your home is located in a southern or western state with moderate year-around temperatures, such heating devices can help provide most of your heating needs.

You can use for fuel the branches and limbs you trim from your trees during seasonal pruning. You can cut down and utilize dead and

Fig. 12-9. Multi-fuel furnaces are available which burn wood or conventional fuels. Check to see if local codes allow them in your area before buying, and have installed units carefully checked for safety. Source: Longwood.

183

TYPE HEATER	ABOVE TOP	FROM FRONT	FROM BACK	FROM SIDES	
Room Heater	36	36	36	36	
Unit Heater	18	48	18	18	
Cook Stove Clay Lined Firepot	30		24	FIRING SIDE 24	OPPOSITE SIDE 18
Cook Stove Unlined Firepot	30		36	36	18

Fig. 12-10. For safety, free-standing stoves should have adequate clearance from combustible materials and should never be installed in closets or alcoves. Minimum clearances (in inches) are shown in the chart. Source: Minn. Energy Agency.

diseased trees. You can also scavenge firewood from dumps and landfills since many localities have now passed ordinances which prohibit burning. The abundance of this type of wood is steadily mounting.

Firewood is often available from industrial sources. It is not uncommon for sawmills, for example, to sell off slabs and other waste wood products at low cost. Power companies, too, often sell trees and branches inexpensively from powerline maintenance programs. But there's more to heating with wood than just felling a tree, cutting it to length and using it as firewood. The type of tree you select, and how you split and store the wood, all have a bearing on the eventual efficiency of your wood stove.

Not all woods produce the same amount of heat. Some are harder to split. Others will vary in the amount of sparks and smoke produced.

WHICH IS BEST FOR FIREWOOD

Softwoods, like pine, fir and spruce, are easy to ignite and burn very fast with a hot flame. But the speed with which softwoods burn is what makes this wood the least desirable firewood. Such a fire needs constant attention and frequent replenishing. On the other hand, a softwood fire can be the perfect answer when you want a warmup fire to simply remove a chill in the air, and then have it burn out so you can leave or retire for the evening.

In general, you should avoid using scrap lumber and refuse. These materials, especially when excessively dry, produce a great deal of sparking which escapes up the flue and becomes a fire hazard.

The best fire—that is, one which is longer-burning with a good amount of heat—is produced by combining softwoods with hardwoods such as oak, maple, birch and ash. The hardwood species burn less vigorously and with a shorter flame; thus, they burn slower. If you want an aroma, add woods from fruit and nut trees to your fire. Apple, cherry, hickory and pecan, for instance, all give off extra pleasant aromas. In most cases, the odor of fruitwood smoke resembles the fragrance of the tree's fruit.

If you buy your firewood, you should know that it is sold by the cord—a stack that measures 4′ × 4′ × 8′. Today a cord of wood sells for anywhere from $35 to $85 or higher (Fig. 12-11), depending upon the wood species and the locale.

The price of firewood alone is ample reason for doing your own cutting. For many homeowners, once they have burned more than a cord of firewood which they've cut themselves, they have almost paid for the chain saw. Given care, a quality chain saw can be used to cut fireplace logs for years.

There aren't any fast and hard rules on how much one will spend on wood. The average home getting most of its heat from wood will burn seven cords a year, according to the U. S. Dept. of Agriculture. Assuming good hardwood is going for $50 per cord and you can get your wood free, then you could pay for a $150 chain saw and a $200 mechanical wood splitter in one year. If you have to buy trees to fell, the payoff won't be as quick.

CUTTING FIREWOOD

Longer logs are considerably cheaper than those which are already cut to fireplace size (by the dealer) and split. Order logs that are economical but also of a length which you can comfortably maneuver. Then simply slice them up into fireplace lengths—most of the time this means 24 inches.

The diameter of the logs which you buy should be governed by your chain saw's capacity. If possible, stick to logs of a diameter that you can slice with a single pass because it makes the job both easier and faster. Newer chain saws can cut logs up to 20″ diameter, and have valuable safety features.

Try to pick out straight-grained, knot-free logs. They are much

Break even price for a cord of various types of wood based on the price of alternate fuels

	Coal	Fuel Oil (No. 2)	Electricity
Cottonwood, basswood, poplar	$37	$40	$42
Alder, aspen, butternut, willow, cedar	$43	$45	$48
Chestnut, sassafras, bald cypress, hemlock, pine	$49	$50	$54
Cherry, elm, magnolia, maple (except sugar), sweetgum, sycamore, tupelo, douglas fir and larch	$54	$55	$61
Ash, birch, hackberry, walnut, tamarack	$61	$63	$66
Beech, hickory (pecan), honey locust, sugar maple and all oak	$67	$70	$70
Black locust	$71	$75	$77
True hickory, dogwood	$75	$80	$84

How to use the table: Any time the price of a full cord for the type of wood available is below that listed in the chart for alternate heat sources, you can save money burning wood. For example, if you have a furnace that uses No. 2 fuel oil, you can save money by burning oak anytime you can purchase it for less than $70 a cord.

Fig. 12-11. These comparisons are based on a selling price of $75/ton for coal, $.40 per gallon for No. 2 fuel oil, and 2¢ per kWh for electricity. A 50% efficiency was assumed for the wood stove, 60% for coal, 65% for No. 2 fuel oil, and 100% efficiency for electricity. Based on calculations using USDA, Forest Service information and tables.

easier to split than those with crooked grain. Also keep in mind that green or wet woods are more easily split than seasoned wood. And softwoods in general split with less effort than hardwoods.

Don't try to split logs until after you have cut them to length simply because short logs are easier to split than long ones.

BENEFITS OF CURING

From 10% to 44% of the heat value of wood can be lost by burning green wood rather than letting it dry to 25% moisture content. Reason? It takes more energy to "evaporate" the extra moisture out of the wood. Green logs are also harder to start and keep burning. Wood dries 10 times as fast through the ends as the sides. Cutting wood to burning length exposes more ends to the air and results in faster drying and lower moisture. After wood is cut to length, splitting logs will allow them to dry half again as fast as the whole log.

Bring 4' lengths to a central location for cutting to length and splitting. While wood may dry slightly faster with the bark removed, it's not necessary to debark your logs (with the exception of diseased elm and oak, which should be debarked to help stop the spread of disease).

STORING TECHNIQUES

The ideal place to store and dry firewood is in an open area with some sort of cover, with the firewood supported by cement blocks or posts. A cover prevents rain and snow from soaking directly into the logs. Open sides insure that the wind, regardless of its direction, will blow through the logs. If the firewood is stacked on the ground, the bottom logs may be lost to rot.

For the best burning, plan to let the wood dry one year. If you live in the South or Southwest you can have acceptable firewood in as little as three months. In the North, plan on a minimum of six months. You can tell if wood is dry by just looking at the end of a log. Green wood shows the annual rings and the saw marks quite plainly. Wood air-dried to 20% moisture will be a dull gray and have lines radiating from the center to the edge. The longer and wider the cracks, the drier the wood.

SPLITTING OPTIONS

Unless you're planning to do a lot of splitting, you can use a 6 lb. or 8 lb. splitting maul with a full length handle. Because of the extra weight and the shape of the head, it can split logs much easier than an axe can. You also can use wedges. If you plan to use firewood for part or all of your home heat, you may want to buy or rent a mechanical splitter.

From a strictly economical point of view, renting is a good option. Many rental stores and chain saw dealers will rent hydraulic log splitters (Fig. 12-12) for $25 to $35 per day. You can cut your logs to length one weekend, rent a log splitter the next weekend, and split and year's supply of firewood or more in one day.

Fig. 12-12. Types of wood splitters include various hydraulic units powered by engines or tractors, cone or screw splitters, and jack-and-blade units. If you can get wood worth $50 a cord free, you can pay for a $150 chainsaw and $200 wood splitter in just one year. Source: Deere & Co.

HYDRAULIC SPLITTERS

Logs to be split are rested on a metal beam or pan. A hydraulic cylinder then pushes the log into a steel wedge to split the wood. Most are designed to handle 24″ or longer logs and have enough power to split knots. Models can be powered by a tractor's hydraulic system or from their own power source. Some are available with a hydraulic jack. After setting the log on the splitter, move away and start the splitting process. Keep hand and arms away while the machine is in operation. Prices for these units range from $300 to $4,000.

CONE OR SCREW SPLITTERS

The log is pushed up to the cone, and the cone screws its way through the log until the log splits (Fig. 12-13). These units are available with their own power source, or they can be mounted onto the rear wheel of an automobile or garden tractor, or they can be attached to a tractor's power takeoff. Prices range from $200 to $400.

Fig. 12-13. Cone or screw splitter. Source: Bark Buster.

Fig. 12-14. Jack and blade splitter. Source: Better Way Products.

JACK AND BLADE SPLITTERS

Logs up to 12″ in diameter and 19″ to 26″ long are set on a stand and jacked into the blade. These units are designed so that every inch you move the jack causes a 2″ separation in the log. Price is about $150. See Fig. 12-14.

Chapter 13
You Can Install an Energy-Efficient Fireplace

You Can Install an Energy-Efficient Fireplace

A number of fireplaces you can buy have built-in heat recovery systems. If you decide to install a fireplace, keep in mind that two keys to increased heating efficiency are: (1) having air for combustion come from outside the home and (2) isolating the fireplace from inside air with glass doors.

WHAT'S AVAILABLE

There is a wide variety of fireplaces you can install. From a do-it-yourselfer's point of view, fireplaces can be broken down into two kinds: those that are difficult to install, and those that are relatively easy to install.

In the former category is the standard masonry fireplace. Masonry fireplaces, besides being costly ($1,500 and up), are difficult to install. They require the skills of a bricklayer and the house may have to be shored up to support the weight of the structure. The semi-fabricated heat circulating unit, another type, is also difficult to install, though it costs less to install and has a much more efficient heat output than the masonry type. Because of the installation problems with the above types, most do-it-yourselfers opt for the prefab fireplace.

Prefab fireplaces are made of steel, with both firebox and flue designed to be rather easily assembled and installed in kit fashion. Units available include those designed to be built into or onto walls, and then trimmed with whatever material you wish.

Cost of a prefab fireplace is perhaps one-third the cost of a standard masonry fireplace. Also, since the units are very light, they can be set on any floor where the framing members are sound.

Most of these units can be located close to combustible walls without fear of fire. They have what is known as a "zero clearance." This is because the unit will be either well insulated or have air chambers which will cool it and eliminate the fire hazard.

Some prefabs simply radiate heat from the fire into the room, while others are designed to circulate the heat. They have openings through which inside or outside air circulates and is routed into the room, sometimes with a fan to help the air along. Built-in or built-on fireplaces are available in firebox sizes ranging from 28" to 48". The fireplace itself is generally another 10" wider.

FREE-STANDING FIREPLACES

The other kind of prefab is the free-standing fireplace (Fig. 13-1). It comes in a wide variety of shapes and colors and may be

Fig. 13-1. Typical free-standing fireplace. This one is electric; gas units are also available and, of course, wood-burning types.

mounted on walls or floors, or hung from ceilings. Sizes run from around 20″ × 20″ to 45″ × 30″. Installation of a freestanding unit is easy. Unless otherwise specified, it must be set back from walls that are combustible.

HOW TO INSTALL A NEW FIREPLACE

Following is an example of what's involved in installing a prefab fireplace. The unit shown is typical of the prefab fireplaces on the market. The 42″ wide insulated unit has a firebox built with a back wall of genuine firebrick to hold and reflect heat, as well as a poured refractory base and porcelainized sidewalls.

It's constructed so no warm room air can escape up the chimney and no heat is wasted. Outside air is drawn into the firebox and used for combustion rather than heated internal air. Cool air from the room is drawn into a heating chamber completely sealed off from the firebox, warmed and recirculated. The glass doors on the unit prevent the escape of warm air while radiating additional heat. As an added energy saver, the simplified circulating air system, in combination with the adjustable front control damper, results in a low burn rate and subsequently more room heat per log.

SELECTING A PREFAB

To get an idea of the hearth size opening you need for an installation, you can use this rule of thumb: Find the dimensions of the room in which you plan to install the fireplace. Add the length to the width, then figure 1″ of fireplace opening for each 1′ of room dimensions. A room 20′ by 22′, for example, gives a total of 42′ and would require a 42″ prefab. Prefabs (Fig. 13-2) can be installed directly over wood floors, and can touch wood framing. When choosing the location for your fireplace, keep window placement, room traffic patterns, and existing construction features in mind. It's best to select a location so the chimney can be installed without cutting rafters or ceiling joists, i.e., where the chimney can pass through ceiling and roof unobstructed. If room space is limited, a corner fireplace will be a space-saver.

When you choose your location, remember that your fireplace opening must not be closer than 3′ to a perpendicular wall of combustible material. With this in mind, frame the opening for the fireplace. If the fireplace will be set on an existing wood floor, buy a piece of sheetmetal 6″ wide and a couple of inches longer than your opening. Place the sheetmetal on the floor so that one edge falls under the unit, the other edge under a hearth of non-combustible material. The hearth is necessary to insure that sparks will not fly out onto the wood floor. The metal strip insures that sparks will not fall between the unit and the hearth.

If you are considering a gas log model, keep in mind that you should pipe in gas lines before you start framing. Use ½″ iron gas pipe with steel or malleable iron fittings. You should also install a child-safe shut-off valve, outside the framing/fireplace enclosure. Remove the outside cover from the fireplace; punch the knock-out plug from the firebox shield; push insulation out of the hole and save for repacking when the pipe is placed. The gas line union is run to a

Fig. 13-2. Typical prefab fireplace before installation. Units generally offer up-to-date, energy-efficient design.

point just outside the fireplace. Then install a nipple of at least 7" to reach inside. Cap the gas line until the log is installed.

PREFAB INSTALLATION

Prefab fireplace installations do not have to be as elaborate as the one shown here (Fig. 13-3). Installing the unit is simple; finishing off the face trim can either be done with easy to use do-it-yourself brick type products, or with a variety of decorative rocks. In this particular installation, the fireplace unit is used as a room divider between kitchen and living room, with the fireplace open to the living room. This unit fits neatly between two posts which rise to the rafters. Sheets of ¾" plywood were used to bridge the 52" gap between the posts. Lightweight stones were applied with a good ceramic tile mastic, then grouted. It's possible to use existing masonry chimneys or prefabricated triple-wall chimneys, which have three pipes-within-pipes, with airspace between. This airspace system of piping keeps the outer pipe cool. The triple-wall chimney fits between framing set on 16" centers.

The first section, or elbow, of the chimney pipe is attached to the unit. Then sections of the fireplace chimney are added as you continue toward the ceiling with the framing. As you add sections of the triple-wall pipe, you must rotate each section until the seam is aligned, and key and notch are mated.

A metal firestop spacer is used on the bottom of any framed opening which the chimney passes through. Although the triple-wall chimney is cool to the touch on the outside, allow a 1" clearance between the chimney and the framing or flooring material. Check this recommendation against your local code. Although 1" clearance is sufficient from a safety standpoint, many cities set their own codes requiring more clearance.

The finished chimney must be at least 3' above the roof cutout, and at least 2' above the highest point of the roof within 10' of the chimney. This is so the chimney top will be sufficiently high from the roof to insure a good draft. Square prefab decorative chimney kits available can be used around the chimney pipe on the roof. If you choose to leave the metal chimney, use flashing, an adapter, a rain collar and a rain cap. See Figs. 13-4 through 13-11.

BASE AND HEARTH

The base for this fireplace unit was first outlined with 4" × 5" beams. Some left-over patio blocks were used for "filler," then the outlined area was filled with cement. The hearth was finished with slate set into the cement. The hearth comes up to within about 1″ of the front of the unit—but not far enough to interfere with the vents which allow room air to be drawn into the unit and reheated (Figs. 13-12 through 13-14).

Fig. 13-3. Inset photos show fireplace unit installed between existing posts. Area to be covered with stone has ¾″ plywood base. A large hearth was designed to balance massive wall. Lightweight rock applied with mastic is supported by nails until mastic dries. Alternate method is to use mortar.

Fig. 13-4. Prefab unit is in place; firestop is installed before installing chimney. Photo perspective is from backside of unit.

Fig. 13-5. First chimney pipe is placed on firestop. Note sheetmetal screws at lower right. Three screws are used to join each section of pipe.

When laying a stone hearth, keep a pail of water and a sponge handy to wash the mortar off the face of the stone. You may have heard that a 5% solution of muriatic acid can be used to clean mortar off brick, stone, or slate. This works only while the mortar is fresh.

Wash with muriatic acid only if the water will not remove mortar; and do so as soon as the mortar has "set" sufficiently so as not to disturb the joints, but before mortar is cured. This will usually be on the same day, and never later than the next day. If you need to use the muriatic for clean-up, remember the acid is extremely caustic. Wear rubber gloves, a shirt to protect your arms, and goggles to keep splashes out of the eyes.

TRIM FACING

Finishing on the framing around your fireplace (Figs. 13-15 through 13-18) can be any material you choose: sheetrock, paneling, brick or stone, or ceramic tile. If you select a combustible material, keep such material a distance of 5″ from the sides and 7″ from the top of the opening. Mantels should not be installed closer than 12″ from the top of the opening.

You may trim the opening with tile and a special heat-resistant adhesive, or with brick by attaching brick ties to the metal edge with sheetmetal screws.

Fig. 13-6. Yardstick was used from first floor to mark center of cutout going through floor above. Plywood is cut out, metal firestop installed.

Fig. 13-7. Alignment is checked through hole to second level. Note boxed hole; this is necessary to carry ceiling joist weight if joist must be cut.

If you choose to make an entire wall of stone, cover the framing around the fireplace with sheetrock or plywood. Then apply self-furring metal lath over the sheetrock/plywood, using 1½″ galvanized roofing nails to secure the lath. Random spacing of these nails is possible on plywood. On sheetrock, nail into the framing since the sheetrock will not support the nails. Nail about every 8″.

Trowel a coat of mortar over this lath, sufficient to cover, usually to a depth of about ½″. Most stone suppliers suggest you wait until this basecoat is dried, or a period of 24 hours, before

Fig. 13-8. Second pipe section of pipe is attached to first, held in place by 3 screws. Note alignment of chimney pipe. Sections are twisted till joints align.

Fig. 13-9. Elbow is attached to pipe, will adjust angle of chimney exit through roof. Elbows come with several different angles for your selection.

Fig. 13-10. Flashing is placed over chimney to cover exit hole through roof. Roof mastic seals flashing/roof joint. You may want to fit pipe through the top of the opening.

Fig. 13-11. Adapter and rain cap are fitted on top chimney. Rain collar fits between the adapter and rain cap.

Fig. 13-12. Designing the hearth. Large pieces of stone are broken to gain irregular shapes. Smaller pieces are easier to level, will aid layout/design of hearth.

applying the stone. It works well to allow the mortar to "set" or become firm (but not dry), then "butter" the stone and apply immediately.

You can mix your own mortar for this or other stone, using a mix of 5 shovels sand, 1 shovel portland, and 1 shovel masonry

Fig. 13-13. Wire lath should be inserted into wood frame, or as adjunct to a stone-only hearth. This lath will tie hearth components together, prevent cracking.

Fig. 13-14. Wooden frame is filled with cement. Stone is laid out to create a pleasing pattern. Small dowel may be used to "strike" joints, smoothing mortar to stone.

cement. A wheelbarrow of at least 3 cu. ft. capacity is a good mortar box. A garden hoe also makes a good mixing device.

Add water to this mix only sparingly, the amount of water depending on the size of the batch you're mixing, the amount of water in the sand, etc. You can buy sand of the grade known as

Fig. 13-15. How to apply face trim. The voids between large rocks are painted with black mastic of the type used to apply artificial brick. This was done in lieu of grouting.

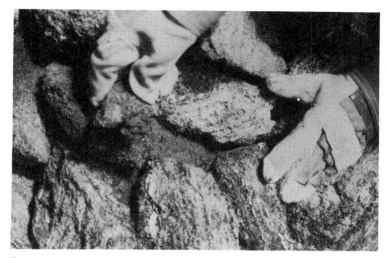

Fig. 13-16. Small or broken rocks, called "rubble," are used to fill gaps between large rocks. You should apply the large rocks to entire wall, then fill gaps.

plaster sand, available in 100-lb. bags from plaster supply houses. Mortar mix should be of the proper stiffness or plasticity to allow good handling on the plaster trowel you use to apply the basecoat.

When installing the furring lath, you'll find that it has a grain or direction to the twist in the lath (Fig. 13-19). Apply this so the projections point upward, to hold the cement to the wall better.

Fig. 13-17. Rock dust is pressed into the black mastic around the small rocks. This treatment results in a wall that appears to be solid stone, rather than grouted.

Fig. 13-18. The mastic/rock/dust application matches the larger rock for finished look.

A plasterer's hawk, or mortar board (Fig. 13-20) can be made by nailing a piece of plywood a foot square onto a bottom of 2″ × 2″ block, or screwed onto a dowel such as an old broomstick. Trowel a supply of the mortar onto this hawk, hold the hawk (the bottom

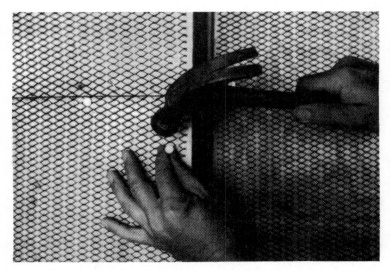

Fig. 13-19. Mortar method of facing. Wirelath is applied over base of plywood, sheetrock, etc. Nail at 8″ intervals with galvanized roofing nails.

206

edge) against the wall, and trowel the mortar upward from the hawk onto the metal lath.

Fireplaces tend to draw a great deal of air from your home. As homes become increasingly tighter in construction, this draft on the fireplace can cause a partial vacuum in the home. This can cause your fire to burn poorly, and give off a good deal of smoke into the room and possibly cause poor venting of fuel fired furnaces. The exterior ducting system of this unit takes care of this problem (Fig. 13-21). Outside air is drawn in and heated, rather than drawing furnace-heated air into the fireplace and up the chimney. This unit also draws

Fig. 13-20. Mortar is best applied with "hawk" or mortarboard held against the lath, trowelled upwards over lath. The technique holds droppings to a minimum.

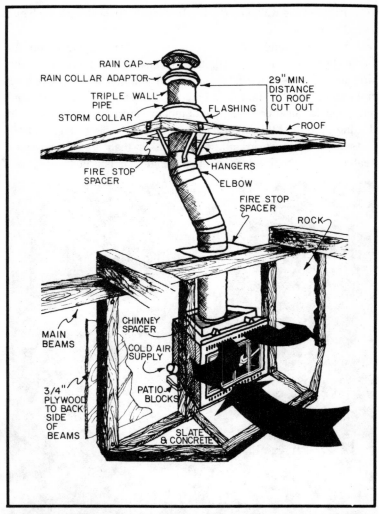

Fig. 13-21. This exterior ducting system eliminates poor venting of fuel and smoke and promotes better burning.

room air into a separate chamber, heats it, and returns it to the room as a supplementary heat source.

The fresh air intake duct in this installation was run up along the chimney, then across at attic level to the soffits. If your fireplace is mounted to an outside wall, simply cut through with a saber saw and duct directly through the wall. Be sure to seal around the duct with caulking.

Chapter 14
Products to Help
You Save More Energy

Products to Help You Save More Energy

More and more products are becoming available to increase the efficiency of your heating and cooling systems. They range from home computers which monitor the performance of heating equipment to sophisticated thermostats and temperature set-back devices. There are even devices which reclaim heat normally lost in furnace operation.

DESCRIPTIONS OF THE PRODUCTS

Because many of the products—and companies—are new, it's wise to investigate thoroughly before buying. At the very least, you want to make sure that a device suits your particular needs and is worth it in the long run.

Home computers, in the future, promise to offer an easy way to keep major appliances operating at peak efficiency to cut your energy costs (Fig. 14-1), chiefly because of a new electronic device called the microprocessor. Already home products are beginning to use microprocessors to replace electro-mechanical and solid-state controls. (A microprocessor, the size of a dime, is a set of silicon chips that accepts inputs, produces predetermined outputs to operate a product and is programmable.)

Personal use computers are already available for home use which consist of a TV screen, typewriter size keyboard and a memory-storage cassette recorder. The units, weighing under 50 lbs., fit on a desk and use programmed tapes.

Fig. 14-1. Personal use computers using microprocessors are available. Fitted with preprogrammed tapes they have the potential to cut energy bills dramatically.

Microprocessors and related electronic control devices also can already be found in appliances (see Chapter 11) and have the potential of trimming your utility bills by letting you conveniently schedule appliance use at non-peak electrical use periods, more accurately matching water levels and appliance cycles to your needs. The appliances also promise fewer and cheaper service bills.

Experts say other home appliances can be adapted to use microprocessors, already in use on calculators, computers and electronic watches. These include furnaces, central and window air conditioners, water softeners and others. While this mini-revolution in the appliance industry promises help in saving energy, other space-age energy savers are also available for installation in your home.

Computerized systems for saving fuel with hot water systems (Fig. 14-2), for example, are already available. In many existing systems the hot water is stopped from circulation whenever the

Fig. 14-2. Computerized systems like this one have the potential of trimming fuel needed for heating homes with hot water by 50%.

thermostat has achieved the desired temperature. The heat (maintained at 170° to 190°F) in the non-circulating water in the heating unit escapes up the chimney as "stack-loss heat."

One computer-like device available correlates heat desired with outside temperature and temperature of hot water in the system and determines what temperature the circulating water should be. It then keeps water circulating constantly, maintaining temperature in the home closer to a constant level. Result is lower fuel consumption.

Automatic thermostat control devices available adjust furnace thermostat settings both up and down automatically when you want, and to the level you desire (Fig. 14-3). The same devices can be used for heating in the winter and cooling in the summer. The units have the potential of knocking up to 15% off home heating costs.

Exact energy savings depend upon your home's design, amount of insulation, of insulation, climate, temperature settings and utility rates. The table (Fig. 14-4) gives you a rough idea of what your potential could be with dial down units. If you live in the Kansas City area, for example, and your control device is set to dial temperature down 10 degrees at night for eight hours you may be able to cut heating bills by 12%. Over an entire $400 heating season, that's an extra $48 in your pocket.

Two types of furnace thermostat devices are available: (1) a converter setback device which works with your existing conventional thermostat, and (2) a replacement setback device designed to replace your present thermostat.

The converter setback device comes in several variations. A two-component version uses a temperature control mounted below

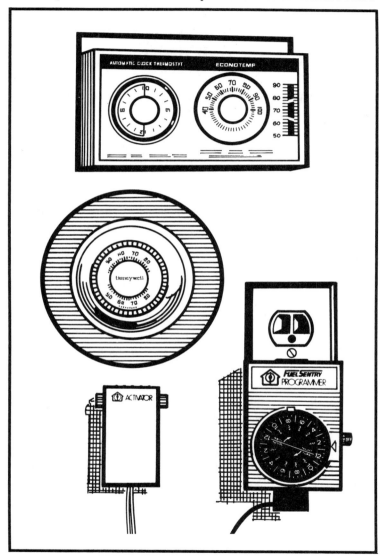

Fig. 14-3. Automatic thermostat controls are available in replacement and converter versions, as shown here. Some are used as "anti-freeze" devices in second homes.

the existing thermostat. Wires, which may or may not be concealed in the wall, connect it to a separate timer unit plugged into a wall outlet. The single-unit version incorporates the timer and temperature control into a single box which attaches to the wall below the thermostat. It runs on self-contained batteries or plugs into a nearby wall unit. Do-it-yourself converter devices generally sell for under $40.

One two-component version available adjusts temperature within a 15°F range. You pre-set a small heating element in the activator component mounted below the thermostat to "fool" it into thinking the room is warmer than it is. The programmer component adjusts temperature to your living schedule.

Some inexpensive converter setback units with fixed 5°F or 10°F setback, have a 32°F low limit. These units are carving out a special niche for themselves as an anti-freeze device in vacation homes and areas such as heated garages.

The replacement setback device is usually more expensive ($75 and up) and more difficult to install. This kind of unit replaces the thermostat entirely and usually requires additional wiring in existing walls. However, these units offer a neater appearance.

To install an automatic clock thermostat, it's first located on an inside wall at a height and location that best represents room temperature. The outer housing is removed, and the thermostat base is positioned and secured on the wall where the wiring comes through. The unit is then connected according to supplied wiring diagram in accordance with local electrical codes. A one-zone room thermostat requires three separate wires for connection to a 24-volt source. With two or three-zone units, the wiring diagram is followed for proper connection to slave units. The last step is adjusting the unit to desired settings.

A knowledgeable homeowner can install these devices. However, if you have any doubt about the procedure, check your plans with a qualified heating controls specialist.

Balancing heat loss with heat supply is another way to cut heating bills. One device available automatically varies timing of furnace flame-on interval to match heat output to weather. It can reduce heating bills an average 15% according to its manufacturer.

A 1" × 3" cylindrical anodized aluminum housing contains a heat loss detector. It mounts outside the house just above the

PERCENT FUEL SAVINGS WITH NIGHT THERMOSTAT SETBACK FROM 75°F

City	8-hour Setback period		16-hour Setback Period	
	5° Setback*	10° Setback*	5° Setback	10° Setback
Atlanta	11	15	22	30
Boston	7	11	14	22
Buffalo	6	10	12	20
Chicago	7	11	14	22
Cincinnati	8	12	16	24
Cleveland	8	12	16	24
Dallas	11	15	22	30
Denver	7	11	14	22
Des Moines	7	11	14	22
Detroit	7	11	14	22
Kansas City	8	12	16	24
Los Angeles	12	16	24	32
Louisville	9	13	18	26
Milwaukee	6	10	12	20
Minneapolis	8	12	16	24
New York City	8	12	16	24
Omaha	7	11	14	22
Philadelphia	8	12	16	24
Pittsburgh	7	11	14	22
Portland	9	13	18	26
Salt Lake City	7	11	14	22
Average	8	12	16	24

*Figures reprinted by permission of the American Society of Heating, Refrigerating and Air-Conditioning Engineers, Inc.

Fig. 14-4. Percent of fuel savings at night with thermostat set back from 75°F.

foundation. A connecting cable, running to available terminals at the furnace, signals flame-on intervals. The unit fits any existing gas-fired forced air or hot water heating system and requires no change to furnace or thermostat.

Thermostatic radiator valves (also called non-electric heating control valves) are available for installing in any hot water or two-pipe steam heating system to effectively control the heating medium in a room, a loop, or a zone for both fuel savings and increased comfort.

Zone control valves prevent overheating to provide substantial fuel savings and, if desired, the temperature setting can be locked or limited. Such valves give 100% shutoff, protect against freezing and backseat open so that heating system need not be drained for repair.

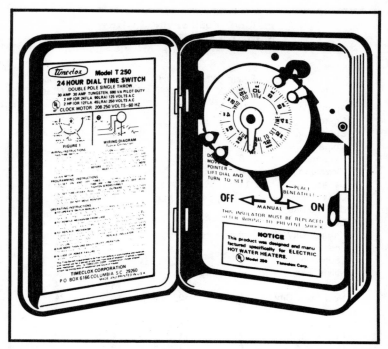

Fig. 14-5. Timers for electric hot water heaters can cut electricity needed by 50% in some cases. You preset units so heater works only when you need hot water.

Usually these are best selected and installed by a qualified heating contractor.

Automatic timers for electric water heaters (Fig. 14-5), say some manufacturers, can cut power needs for heating water by 50% or more. Electric water heaters rank second only to home heating and cooling systems in energy consumption. Units automatically turn the water heater on and off, according to time periods you set. By restricting operation to when hot water is normally needed (two hours in morning and two hours in evening), power use drops while the average family still gets ample hot water. The units are relatively inexpensive. Some manufacturers promise a minimum monthly savings of $10 when basic instructions for economy operation are followed.

Motorized flue dampers (Fig. 14-6) can capture heat otherwise wasted from heating units. They are available on new furnaces, or as separate add-on packages. One vent damper mounts to the flue of the furnace and automatically opens and closes it when the thermostat calls for heat. The automatic flue damper, says one firm, is capable of saving up to 16% on a season's heating bill.

It cuts the operating cost of an indoor furnace by improving year-around utilization efficiency in two ways. First, closing the flue when the furnace isn't operating prevents indoor air from escaping up the chimney. Second, closing the flue immediately after the gas shuts off traps the heat stored in the hot heat exchangers, preventing it from escaping up the chimney and requiring less time for warm up when the thermostat calls for heat. The stainless steel damper is motor driven to the closed position and has a safety switch which prevents the gas valve from operating unless the vent is fully open.

Other motorized flue dampers are available for oil-fired furnaces. One, for example, is made of heavy cast iron and fits 6″ to 10″

Fig. 14-6. Motorized flue dampers automatically open and close the furnace flue to prevent heat loss up chimney and cut warm-up time when furnace cycles.

flues. Models are available through heating equipment dealers and installers.

Wood burning "helper" units (Fig. 14-7) with forced air fans are also worth considering. The helper units, say manufacturers, have the potential of supplying up to 75% or more of your home heating Btu's if attended regularly and stoked properly.

Most manufacturers which make a helper unit also make combination wood/oil or wood/coal burning furnaces. Therefore, a lot of years of experience has gone into making them efficient and reliable.

A handyman can buy, cart in and install a helper-type wood-burning furnace to supplement an existing heating system for a total price of between $600 and $1,200. Price depends upon brand, size and hardware needed to mate the new to the existing furnace. Sheet metal piping, collars, elbows and self-tapping chuck-head sheetmetal screws to do the job are available at building material centers.

Makers selling helper wood furnaces also supply installation instructions and bills of materials upon request. Some also offer their dealers and direct consumer buyers free phone consultation on installation, and will make up any kit or fitting you ask for at low cost. Check to see if the unit you are considering is UL listed. Some other things to watch for:

Keep in mind that if heated air from the helper unit feeds into the furnace blower unit, at 300°F ambient temperature can cook the blower's electric motor.

If it feeds into the furnace plenum, 300°F air going into the duct system may present a fire hazard. Gas-designed furnaces have high limit switches that immediately shut off fuel if air temperature exceeds 200°F.

When a helper unit's combustion chamber fails, it also could deliver carbon monoxide into the whole house. Also, if you're looking at units which deliver heated air to the furnace plenum, keep in mind this is the normal location of an air conditioning coil and may be too hot for the coil. With any helper unit, a fail-safe thermostat control is essential; a smoke detector is also a worthwhile accessory.

You should look at construction, and Btu output in particular, when buying a helper furnace. Heat output when stoked up should be in the upper half of the 50,000 to 100,000 Btu range. Be careful about how the maker rates the output and try to accurately pinpoint average Btu output with a normal wood burn.

For instance, in one model's 16″ × 24″ firebox, stacking three 9″ dia. by 21″ logs with a bright burn will produce about 85,000 usable Btu's with a small blower. Electric squirrel-cage direct drive blowers of 1/3 to 1/6-hp will deliver 750 to 1,500 cfm of air. This is plenty to propel air around the heat box and into heat ducts.

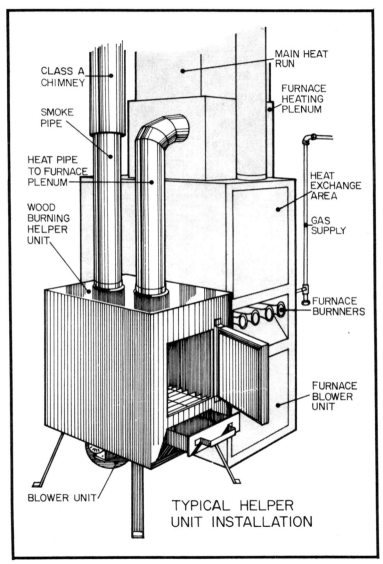

Fig. 14-7. Typical helper unit installation.

Your furnace should have certain standard equipment supplied to be a good buy: automatic damper control to vary the burning rate as the fire alternately takes off, then recedes; blower system, either built-in or in side-by-side mounted plenum; electrical controls; good-size bottom ash box, and heavy gauge construction. Check for a 22 to 25 gauge steel furnace cabinet and a 9 to 12 gauge cast steel firebox, with 1" or better cast iron grates and liners of 2" or better firebrick liners.

A controversy exists over whether cast iron or firebrick is better for reliable, long-lasting liner material. While brick has a well-deserved reputation for retaining heat and protecting corrosive steel surfaces, cast iron liners also prove to be long-wearing and are simple to replace if needed.

While many manufacturers insist upon caulked or asbestos-corded airtight doors, others like a small air bleed. Some design units with non-airtight doors to prevent gas build-up explosions. Reason: when a fire takes off, unburned gases can build up. If a fire door is opened, the sudden in-rush of oxygen may set off a blast.

Delivered cost of a furnace depends on features, construction, and, therefore, weight. Helper furnaces have a 300- to 500-lb. dry weight, so it makes sense to try to find a manufacturer nearby if you want to buy f.o.b. at the factory. Freight is generally built into a dealer's price.

But don't buy on price alone. The heavier the furnace construction, the longer it will last.

The home handyman who wants to invest a day or day-and-a-half in a cost-saving project can mate any of various woodburning "helper" furnaces into existing forced-air furnace systems, be it oil, gas, electric or a heat pump.

The main difference in systems is the position of blower (if it has one), placement of the helper unit, and the amount of materials you'll have to buy to complete the mating installation. Some units use a separate blower box. Some are available which have the blower attached directly to the helper unit.

A number of companies manufacturing wood heating units will either have a "helper" unit, or be able to suggest how their units can be adapted to your present furnace system. Also check with a qualified heating specialist both before and after installing helper units, especially concerning hook-up procedures.

Heat reclaimers (Fig. 14-8) can also make a significant difference in your fuel bills. Heat reclaimers "scrub" additional heat from your heating system. Installed in the exhaust flue of furnaces, fireplaces, heaters or stoves, they contain a cluster of tubes. These tubes capture heat from combustion exhaust. The reclaimed heat can then be redirected to supplement the overall heating system or to warm a separate room or "cold spot." When the reclaimed heat is ducted through walls or ceiling, be sure to provide an easy "return path" back to the furnace area (Fig. 14-9).

BYPASS TYPE HEAT RECLAIMER INSTALLATION

The heat reclaimer (Fig. 14-10) is installed with a dampered duct between the warm air plenum and the cold air return. This type

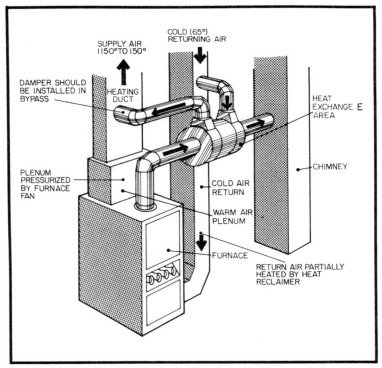

Fig. 14-8. Some heat reclaimers mount into the vent connector, then reconnect into the chimney. The heat reclaimer and bypass ducts take heat from the products of combustion in the vent connector. The added heat is mixed with the cold air return flow. In using this type of hardware, the stack temperature will be higher because warmer air is returned to the furnace. Note: bypass should be closed when only furnace is used, or when using air conditioning.

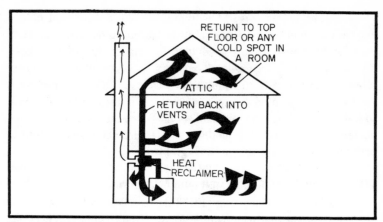

Fig. 14-9. Heat from reclaimers can be directed into attic (finished space only), directed through ducts to heat main floor, or to a cold area in the basement.

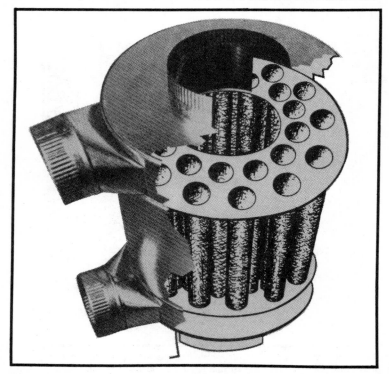

Fig. 14-10. Examples of heat reclaimers. This is a cutaway view of a unit which uses 24 exchanger tubes on outside of stack. Models are available for use on furnaces using oil, wood or coal and free-standing stoves, fireplaces and space heaters.

can cause excessive plenum chamber temperatures due to recirculation through the bypass duct. First, close the bypass damper completely, then check the temperature rise through furnace. Slowly open the bypass damper, frequently checking plenum temperature. When plenum temperature starts to rise, lock and mark damper position for future reference. (If on an air conditioning job, the damper should be closed for cooling mode.)

If moisture drips from heat reclaimer when the system is working, better remove the heat reclaimer. The stack temperature in the vent connector between the heat reclaimer and the chimney should be above 300°F. Poor venting would occur and the moisture would soon cause rusting and leaking in the heat reclaimer.

For maximum operating safety, home heating experts caution that these products must be properly matched to your heating

Fig. 14-11. This heat exchanger is made to install on any furnace, boiler, free-standing fireplace or woodburner. Finished in black enamel, it fits a standard 7″ flue pipe and adapts to other sizes.

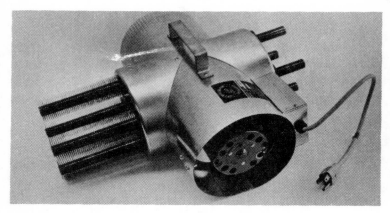

Fig. 14-12. This unit claims recovery up to 15,00 Btu's per hour.

system and correctly wired and installed. If you don't hire a certified technician to install the units, you should double check your plans with a home heating technician to make sure the installation meets local codes and is safe under all conditions.

Heat reclaimers (Fig. 14-11) work best on heating systems with high flue tempratures. These are wood-burning and oil-burning units. Because a gas-fired system requires a relatively high stack temperature to exhaust properly, you should check the feasibility of the reclaimer/gas-fire installation with your local heating inspector, and have the installation and finished job inspected. Make certain the stack temperature on a gas-fired unit is not lower than 300°F after the draft hood since poor venting and carbon monoxide formation is possible at lower temperatures.

Directions for installing these devices (Fig. 14-12) come with the units. However, most units install in-line on the vent connector or stack of your heater/furnace. Best advice is to check with a qualified heating system specialist.

Chapter 15
Energy Savers You
Can Experiment With

Energy Savers You Can Experiment With

Besides the ways to save energy already covered, there are still other ways to save even more. You can decorate your home with an eye to energy efficiency, as well as take advantage of energy-saving landscaping. And, if you're the experimenting type, you can try your hand at using sun power to cut down energy costs.

IDEAS ON FURNISHINGS

The type and arrangement of furnishings can actually help you save energy. Place furniture far enough away from radiators so it doesn't block warm air flow, or cold air returns. Also make sure radiator covers do not restrict heating circulation. If your decor demands covers, make sure that the kind you get has an area that is at least three-quarters open. It is also a good idea to keep the covers clean, both inside and out. Figures 15-1 through 15-4 demonstrate several types of energy-saving furnishings.

If you have a choice for floor covering, use carpeting. This has a higher insulation value than any other kind of floor covering. Of the three common carpet materials available (wool, acrylics and nylon) the best in terms of insulative value are wool and acrylic.

In Chapter 4, the importance of storm windows was pointed out. Solid shades can also help prevent heat loss through windows by over 30%. In the summer they can cut air conditioning costs by one-fifth.

Fig. 15-1. Window well covers, such as this one from BPQ Industries, keep wind and rain out, help save energy.

Fig. 15-2. Drapes by Sherwin-Williams combine wood strips and fabric to provide light and heat control to help save energy.

Fig. 15-3. Do-it-yourself kits are available to deflect the sun's heat before it reaches windows and saves air conditioning dollars. This kit, from Reynolds Metals, uses Owens-Corning solar screening. Photo by courtesy of Reynolds Metals Co.

The bottoms of the draperies should be at least 8″ above radiators or registers so heat flow isn't inhibited; otherwise, deflectors can be used to route heat into the room. If you have baseboard heaters, position the bottoms at least 4″ from them. Drapes should also be closed off at the top with a valance or other arrangement. Normally draperies are set 3″ off the wall. Warm air finds its way behind the draperies from the top, is cooled by window glass, and comes out the bottom.

ENERGY-SAVING LANDSCAPING

Summer sun beating down on your house and winter winds buffeting it can make cooling and heating systems work harder. Landscaping can reduce this assault on your energy producing machinery (Fig. 15-5).

In winter, windbreaks can be very effective. In cold climates, the most popular windbreak tree is the evergreen, but the trees should be planted in a certain way. The north and west sides of the house usually get the most wind. Plant trees in an L-shape configuration to protect them. If you have space, three rows of evergreens planted 14' apart, is effective.

Extend the lines of trees in a L shape around the northwest side, with the middle row of trees planted so they close the gaps between the flanking rows. The ends of the L should extend 50' beyond the ends of the house on both north and west sides. This will keep drifting snow to a minimum.

Fig. 15-4. Energy-saving shutter-blinds are made by several companies. This unit, of vinyl, from Sunega Assoc., helps reduce heating and cooling costs.

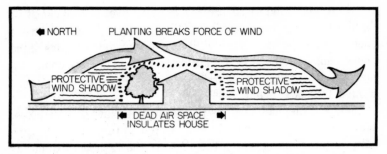

Fig. 15-5. Landscaping can mean energy savings to your homestead.

If you wish you can use other types of trees for windbreaks. Hemlock, spruce and fir are all suitable. You shouldn't choose trees that don't grow close to the ground, such as pine. Smaller evergreens can also be put in next to the house. They help provide insulation by creating a dead air space and also protect against wind.

If your lot is small, you can use two rows of evergreens planted alternately so they form a solid line of greenery. If your property prohibits a windbreak, a high fence can be installed as a substitute.

To keep summer sun from boosting air conditioning costs, use shade trees. Trees that shed their leaves in fall are best, because these allow sun to filter through in winter. Many types are suitable, including red, Norway and sugar maples. These can stand up to bad weather, but provide good shade in summer.

These trees should be planted on the west and east sides of the home so their shadows should fall across the roof. To get an idea of where to plant them, get a pole the approximate height of the full grown tree (or trees) and experiment with it in various positions to see where the shadow falls.

Other greenery that can be used to save energy includes vines, such as wisteria, bittersweet and Boston ivy. These absorb and reflect the sun in the summer, but lose their leaves in winter and let the sun's rays warm the house.

USING SUN POWER

Of all the alternative sources of energy that many will have to be considering over the next 50 years, one of the most promising is solar energy. Energy from the sun is free, and also abundant. Some experts say that enough energy is beamed from the sun every 15 minutes to provide all the earth's needs for an entire year.

While the use of solar energy must still be considered in its infant state, it is being used successfully in some areas of the country. Good old American enterprise guarantees that the equipment will get better and better, the savings greater.

If you want to get a first-hand introduction to using sun power, you can build your own solar collector to tie into your heating system. But before you do, a basic understanding of a solar energy system is required.

There are four basic parts to a solar energy system: (1) a collector, which collects the solar energy; (2) an energy storage unit; (3) a distribution system; and (4) an auxiliary heating system (no current solar system so far can provide 100% of home energy needs).

In general, the system works like this. Solar radiation is absorbed by the collector, transferred to the storage unit by means of pipes, and then distributed to the point of use. The performance of each phase of the operation is maintained by automatic or manual controls.

COLLECTORS

This is the heart of a solar energy system. Today there are two major types of solar collectors in use: the focusing type and flat plate type. Focusing collectors use mirrored surfaces to concentrate solar rays to gain temperatures up to several thousand degrees. However, the focusing collector requires a tracking system to keep it aimed at the sun, and it does not function well when skies are even slightly overcast.

The flat plate system does not concentrate heat, but it has several advantages for home application: it does not need to track the sun; it collects some heat on slightly overcast days; it's cheaply and easily built; and it has a relatively high collection efficiency. For these reasons, flat plate collectors are most commonly used in industry and by the amateur solar experimenter.

Either liquid or air can be used as a vehicle to transfer heat from the flat plate collector to the home. When water or other fluids are used, you need a hot-water flow distribution system, storage tank, circulating pump, flow controls and a water-to-air heat exchanger to extract heat from fluid.

Using air for heat transmission eliminates the possibility of collector freeze-up or possible contamination of the home water supply from anti-freeze. In this system air is heated in the collector, then moved by blowers into a heat exchanger positioned in the ducts of the warm air system of the home. Water heated in the exchanger is used for supplemental water heating. The hot air is then moved through a bin of rocks for storage and home heating.

At this stage of development, experts believe that you can aim for a solar collector input of 40% to 50% of your total heating requirements. A total solar system, they admit, would be extremely costly. Tests at the Langley Research Center, NASA's testing facility at Hampton, Va., show that to provide 40% of your home's heating needs in that climate you'll need collector surface equal to one-third the floorspace of your home. For a 1,500 sq. ft. house, you would need 500 sq. ft. of collector surface.

Solar collectors should be placed facing south and, if roof mounted, installed with the existing slope of the roof. The ideal angle to the sun is the latitude in your area plus 20°. Work at Langley indicates that raising and bracing collectors to the proper angle on an existing roof is not worth the extra work and expense. Ground-mounted units may easily be positioned to the correct angle.

THINK SMALL

The ideal solar system, researchers admit, is one in which the collector and building are designed as a single solar unit.

One Chicago firm's solar home, for example, incorporates collectors in a roof which is built at the proper angle to the sun. The home has 6″ of insulation in walls and 12″ in ceilings, and uses triple-paned windows. To cut heat loss, the houses are built with woods or other windbreaks to the north and earth berms, or mounds, against their bottom portion.

The do-it-yourself collector shown here (Fig. 15-6) is a duplicate of the collector system the firm incorporates into the roofs of their homes. At this point in time, the best advice for solar seems to be: think small! The smaller the area you have to heat, the more feasible solar becomes.

When the collector shown is incorporated into a roof, 2 × 10's are used for rafters. The space between the 2 × 10's is filled with insulation up to a 1″ × 2″ batten. Tempered hardboard is installed over the battens (and between the rafters) and painted black. The roof collector is covered with rigid fiberglass to form both the

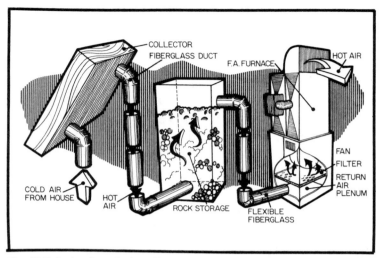

Fig. 15-6. Instructions for installing a thermal flatplate collector.

collector and the finished roof (Fig. 15-7). A heat exchanger is installed in heat ducts to heat water.

This system, in tests, has provided 60% to 70% of winter heating required in the Chicago area. The cheapest solar system is one where you understand solar heating principles enough to manually adjust the flow of solar heat. Automatic controls, however, are available which operate with differential thermostats.

A rock repository for storing heat is often a feature of a solar system (Fig. 15-8).

WHAT YOU CAN BUY

The U. S. Research and Development Administration report lists these solar energy applications as being feasible today for active systems (those employing heat exchangers, blowers, differential thermostats, etc.): hot water heat, supplemental forced air heat, heating swimming pools, and air conditioning. For passive systems, the list includes solar greenhouse and room or area heating.

You can now buy solar hot-water heaters (Fig. 15-9) in the $2,000 to $2,500 range. A number of companies have units which use a flat plate collector. Water flows from collectors to a special water storage tank. When you turn your faucet on, hot water flows from the solar tank to the conventional water heater. Figure 15-10 shows a flat plate collector used in conjunction with a water heater.

STEP 1 Building The Frame

A. Cut two 2x10s for top and bottom plates (lengths will be a 4' increment).
B. Cut four 2x10s, 7'9" long for studs. Cut 10"x8" opening near one end for air passage.
C. Space studs at 16" centers with alternating openings as shown. Nail with 8d common nails.
D. Nail 4'x8'x⅜" plywood on top of frame with 4d common nails.
E. At end modules only: cut 10" diameter hole for connection to supply or return air ducts.
F. Turn assembly over.

STEP 2 Styrofoam Insulating

A. Cut pieces of 1½" thick Styrofoam insulation to fit each space between studs. Glue to plywood back with Styrofoam mastic No. 11.
B. Cut more pieces of 1½" thick Styrofoam for all edges exposed to cold. Glue to 2x10s with same mastic.
C. Paint everything (inside, outside, back) with flat black paint. (One coat primer, one or two coats finish.) Let dry per instructions on paint can.

STEP 3 Add Absorber Plate

A. Run a bead of caulking over exposed edges of 2x10s.
B. Cut 20" wide aluminum flashing to length of collector. Wash both faces of metal with vinegar; rinse with water. Paint both faces with Rustoleum Primer, then paint with Rustoleum #412 Flat Black. Let dry.
C. Tack down first strip of flashing as shown with galvanized roofing nails. Caulk at top edge.
D. Tack down second strip with 1" lap over first strip, caulk.
E. Repeat for third through fifth strips.
F. Caulk continuously over all nailed areas. **Be sure to cover all nail holes.**

STEP 4 Sun-Lite Covering

A. Nail 1x2s, painted flat black, over caulking with 4d common nails.
B. Run a bead of caulking over 2" face of all 1x2s.
C. Tack a 4'x8' sheet of "Sun-Lite" solar collector material over caulked 1x2s with galvanized roofing nails.
D. Run a bead of caulking over all nailed areas.
E. Repeat steps A through D for second layer of "Sun-Lite."
F. Nail 1x2s, painted flat black over caulked 1x2s with galvanized roofing nails.
(Note: **Now position the collector and hook up to forced air furnace.**)

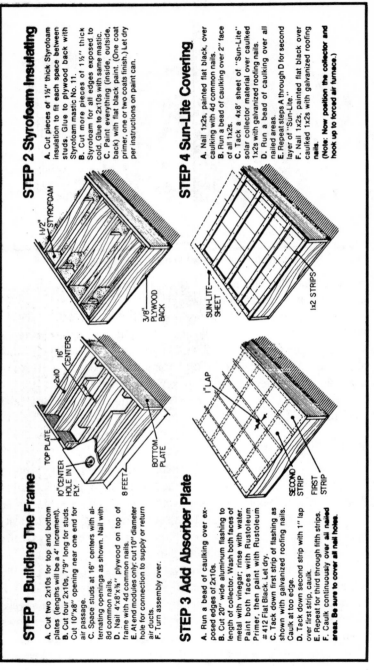

Fig. 15-7. Instructions for building frame for collector to be hooked up to forced air furnace.

234

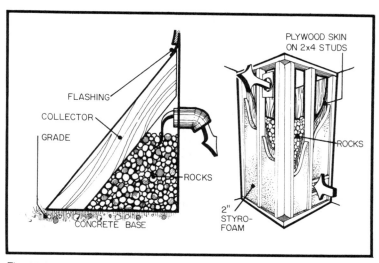

Fig. 15-8. Heat from the sun is stored in rock repository.

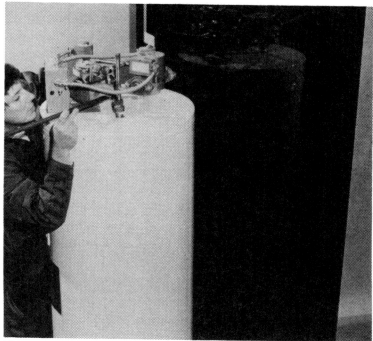

Fig. 15-9. Solar tap water system by PPG consists of water storage tank and collector. It installs with less than an hour's interruption to the home's hot water supply and saves up to 70% on water heating bills.

One system uses four plate collectors and a 52-gal. storage tank to supply up to 80 gal. of hot water daily. Since the unit heats the water directly, rather than heating another fluid and transferring the heat to the water via converters or exchangers, collectors are drained automatically when cold weather hits.

Another company sells collectors for a water heating system at $10 to $14 per sq. ft. as a building block for dealers or handymen. Another company sells a package of four solar collectors, with blower unit, for under $1,000. With this basic package, you can experiment with solar heating on a low-buck basis.

As other sources of energy, wind and water power may be used, and both are susceptible to do-it-yourself installation, though at the present time their appeal would seem to be restricted.

Water Power

To install a water power system, you must have a running stream near your property, ideally a small waterfall. The flow of this water produces power which is turned into usable energy by a variety of devices.

One such is the hydroelectric turbine. Cost of the smallest unit you can buy is over $4,000 and will produce only around 500 watts of power. As you go up the scale in size, though, performance increases dramatically. For example, a turbine that costs around $4,500 will produce 2,000 watts. When you get to units that cost over $7,000 you can produce around 10,00 watts.

Originally expensive, water power can save in the long run. For example if you could get by with a 10,000 watt unit and it saved you $50 or $60 a month in power costs, you could have your money back in 15 years or so. Of course, some appliances, such as a range which requires over 12,000 watts, would probably make a water power system impractical for most.

Fig. 15-10. The flat plate collector is used in conjunction with Lennox's water heater.

Fig. 15-11. Cutaway view of the Lennox flat plate solar collector.

Wind Power

Windpower is the other system of interest to do-it-yourself energy savers. However it has one big drawback: it's expensive. A complete system can cost $15,000.

Most people probably think of a wind power energy system as a propeller and some sort of wheel to produce power. Actually, six essentials are required for a complete system.

It must contain a propeller which is mounted on a tower, high enough so it can catch the wind. A generator to produce the electricity is needed, as are special lead-acid batteries to store the power. Also, converters are required to change the power, which is stored as DC (direct current) to AC (alternating current) used by most homes. Finally, there must be some sort of back-up system to produce power when the batteries are depleted, after a string of calm, windless days.

While expensive, the wind power system can pay dividends over the long run in a remote site where power hookup to a utility company is impossible.

Index

Illustration Credits

1-1: Gas Utility Industry
1-2: American Society Heating,
   Refrigeration and Air Conditioning Engineers
1-3: US Department of Commerce, Owens-Corning
1-4: Owens-Corning
1-5: Chevron USA
1-6: Chevron USA
1-7: Owens Corning
1-8: Owens Corning
2-1: Minnesota Energy Agency
2-2: Owens-Corning
2-3: (series thru 2-7) Certainteed Corporation
2-8: Harry Kalmus
2-9: (series) Johns-Manville
3-1: (series) Gary Branson
3-2: (series) Maize Photography
3-3: (series) Benchmark Doors
4-1: Dow-Corning
4-2: (series 1-4) Gary Branson
4-3: Arnold Romney
4-4: (1&2) Gary Branson
4-5: Arnold Romney
4-6: Arnold Romney
4-7: Gary Branson
5-1: Triangle Engineering
5-2: Leigh Products
5-3: Leigh Products
5-4: Leigh Products
5-4A: Leigh Products
5-5: Leigh Products
5-6: (series, 5-6 thru 5-11) Gary Branson
6-1: US Department of Commerce
6-2: McGraw Edison
6-3: McGraw Edison
6-4: (series 6-4 thru 6-14) McGraw Edison
7-1: Fred Dingler
7-2: Fred Dingler
7-3: Mort Schultz
7-4: Mort Schultz
7-5: Mort Schultz
7-6: Ron Chamberlain
7-7: Ron Chamberlain
7-7A: Mort Schultz
7-8: Mort Schultz
7-9: Mort Schultz
7-10: Mort Schultz

8-1: John Nelson
8-2: Air Conditioning and Refrigeration Institute
8-3: Air Conditioning and Refrigeration Institute
8-4: Comfort Enterprises & Co.
8-5: Comfort Enterprises & Co.

8-6: Comfort Enterprises & Co.
9-1: York Division of Borg-Warner
9-2: York Division of Borg-Warner
9-3: York Division of Borg-Warner
10-1: Ron Chamberlain
10-2: Eswa Industries
10-3: Aztec Ind.
10-4: Emerson Chromalox
10-5: Mort Schultz
10-6: Koehring Corp. Art alternatives
   to photos by Ron Chamberlain
10-7: John Deere
11-1: (series) Sears
11-2: Whirlpool Corp.
11-3: Litton Ind.
11-4: General Electric
11-5: General Electric
11-6: Johnson Industries
12-1: Fireplace Grate Heat Co.
12-2: Marline Metalcraft
12-3: Eagle Industries
12-3A: El Fuego
12-4: Bennett-Ireland
12-5: Jotul, Shenandoah, Silver Star (Series)
12-6: Longwood
12-7: Minnesota Energy Agency
12-7A: USDA, Forest Service
12-8: Deere and Co., Bark Buster (series)
12-9: Better Way Products
13-1: Stoneridge Mfg. Co, Inc.
13-2: Majestic
13-3 thru 13-21: Terry Redlin
14-1: Paul Sansale
14-2: John Nelson
14-3: John Nelson
14-4: John Nelson
14-5: John Nelson
14-6: Fred Dingler
14-7: Fred Dingler
14-8: Fred Dingler
14-9: Gateway Industries
14-10: General Machinery
14-11: Isothermics
15-1: BPQ Industries
15-2: Sherwin-Williams
15-3: Reynolds Metals
15-4: Sunega Associates
15-5: Ron Chamberlain
15-6: Ron Chamberlain
15-7: Ron Chamberlain
15-8: PPG
15-9: Lennox